CHUCK YEAGER

ALSO BY DON KEITH

CHUCK YEAGER

World War II Fighter Pilot

DON KEITH

CALIBER

CALIBER

an imprint of Penguin Random House LLC
penguinrandomhouse.com

DUTTON and the D colophon are registered trademarks
of Penguin Random House LLC.

Images from U.S. Air Force

LIBRARY OF CONGRESS CATALOGING-IN-PUBLICATION DATA

Names: Keith, Don, 1947–author.
Title: Chuck Yeager: World War II fighter pilot / Don Keith.
Description: [New York]: Dutton Caliber, [2022]
Identifiers: LCCN 2022026325 (print) | LCCN 2022026326 (ebook) |
ISBN 9780593187272 (trade paperback) | ISBN 9780593187289 (ebook)
Subjects: LCSH: Yeager, Chuck, 1923–2020. | United States. Army Air Forces.
Fighter Squadron, 363rd–Biography. | Fighter pilots—United States—Biography. |
Mustang (Fighter plane). | World War, 1939–1945—Campaigns—Western Front. |
World War, 1939–1945—Aerial operations, American. |
World War, 1939–1945—Regimental histories—United States.
Classification: LCC D790.262 363rd 2022 (print) | LCC D790.262 363rd (ebook) |
DDC 940.54/4973092 [B]—dc23/eng/20220630
LC record available at https://lccn.loc.gov/2022026325
LC ebook record available at https://lccn.loc.gov/2022026326

Printed in the United States of America

2nd Printing

★ CONTENTS ★

CHUCK YEAGER

PROLOGUE

*All I know is I worked my tail off learning to fly. If there is
such a thing as the right stuff in piloting, then it is experience. The secret to my success was that somehow I always
managed to live to fly another day.*

—Charles E. "Chuck" Yeager

For a stretch of more than sixty years, Charles Elwood
Yeager was one of the more recognized figures on the planet.
He was a regular guest on television, including appearances on *What's My Line?*, *This Is Your Life*, *The Tonight Show
Starring Johnny Carson*, and *The David Letterman Show*, and
even had brief camera time in sitcoms, such as *I Dream of Jean-
nie*. He was featured in scores of commercials and print ads for
General Motors and ACDelco. He made cameo appearances in
such movies as *The Right Stuff* (in which he also did most of the
flying and had a bit part as the bartender at a watering hole
frequented by Air Force test pilots) and in *Smokey and the Ban-
dit II*. His real-world experiences as a daring and colorful test
pilot were featured in both the nonfiction work *The Right Stuff*
by Tom Wolfe and the movie of the same name based on the
book. Yeager was portrayed in the film by actor Sam Shepard,

who received an Academy Award nomination as Best Supporting Actor for his interpretation. (Shepard was the son of a US Army officer and World War II bomber pilot but also had a well-publicized fear of flying.) Yeager himself had almost three dozen film credits.

Yeager twice drove the pace car to start the Indianapolis 500 motor race. He served as consultant for three flight simulator video games, each of which bore his name in their titles. One became Electronic Arts' best-selling video game of 1987. On a more serious note, President Ronald Reagan appointed Yeager to the Rogers Commission, tasked with investigating the space shuttle *Challenger* disaster in January 1986.

President Gerald Ford presented him with the Congressional Silver Medal, generally considered to be the noncombat equivalent to the Medal of Honor. He was inducted into the National Aviation Hall of Fame, the International Air & Space Hall of Fame, the California Hall of Fame, and the Aerospace Walk of Honor.

In his home state of West Virginia, the airport at Charleston was dubbed Yeager Airport, and the Interstate 77 bridge over the Kanawha River was also named in his honor. Several stretches of highway around the state also bear his name. And though he never attended college, Marshall University dubbed its top academic scholarship program the Society of Yeager Scholars.

He was also a best-selling author. His life story, *Yeager: An Autobiography*, was a long-term success, as was a follow-up book, *Press On!: Further Adventures in the Good Life*.

Chuck Yeager was a likable, charismatic, and colorful figure, a self-described individualist. His tendency to be plainspoken and incisive rubbed some in the military the wrong way but only helped endear him to the general public. The event that truly put him into the limelight—and earned him a place in the script for *The Right Stuff*—came on October 14, 1947, above the high desert of central Southern California.

On that day Yeager accomplished something many thought impossible and everyone knew to be highly dangerous. He piloted a rocket-powered aircraft—dropped from the belly of a B-29 bomber—to a speed of more than 660 miles per hour, swifter than the speed of sound at that altitude and faster than any human being had ever moved on purpose. The "sound barrier" had long terrified but fascinated engineers and pilots. Many scientists, without equivocation, predicted an aircraft approaching and then flying through that speed point would simply come apart, disintegrating in midair due to violent shock waves buffeting the plane.

But then, with Chuck Yeager at the controls of that bottle rocket of an airplane—a Bell X-1 that Yeager had named *Glamorous Glennis* after his wife, as he did many of the planes he flew in his lifetime—there was proof that such a catastrophe could be avoided after all if the aircraft was properly designed and flown. It was a bumpy ride all right, but he had demonstrated once and for all that—with the specific aeronautical design and a competent pilot who could make the appropriate adjustments at the right time—Mach 1 was no barrier at all. It was merely another tick on a Machmeter.

For the first known time in history, people on the ground heard the thunder of a sonic boom from an aircraft going faster than sound travels—a sound that Yeager himself could not hear in the X-1's cockpit because the shock wave was directed downward, toward the ground.

The Air Force managed to keep the accomplishment a secret for more than half a year, but when the news broke, along with the details about the man who was in the cockpit that day, Chuck Yeager's celebrity was assured, right alongside his place in history. The world was looking for heroes. America was anxious for any accomplishment that showed scientific or military advances in response to other nations that were, just ahead of the Cold War, challenging US dominance. The brave but nonchalant, self-effacing guy with the West Virginia drawl was almost immediately a national folk hero.

The legend would only grow as people learned more about the background to the story. How Yeager was chosen for the job even though he had no formal education beyond high school. All the other candidates were graduate engineers. How the civilian pilot who had done preliminary work with the X-1 had demanded more money, a huge bonus, for assuming the risk in attempting to jet through the sound barrier. However, Chuck Yeager, as an Air Force pilot, would necessarily do it on the cheap. And later the public would hear the story of just how painful that brief sojourn over the desert was. How Chuck and Glennis had ridden their horses down to a local bar two nights before the X-1 flight. On the way back to the barn, Chuck was thrown from his horse, badly breaking two ribs. Yet he still managed to climb into the aircraft and, because of his injuries, use a makeshift broom handle lever to get the door closed and latched and then pilot the craft through Mach 1 and into history.

Then, later, just for good measure, he flew the X-1 at 2.5 times the speed of sound.

Yeager continued his Air Force career in spectacular fashion after the record-breaking feat, holding command positions in both the Korean conflict and the Vietnam War, along with the Cold War. He flew more than two hundred combat missions over Vietnam and other spots in Southeast Asia. He was also commandant of the US Air Force Aerospace Research Pilot School, responsible for turning out astronauts for the Air Force and the nation's space program. However, with no college degree, he was never eligible to become an astronaut like the men whose training he oversaw.

In October 1997, at the age of seventy-four, Yeager was in the pilot's seat of a F-15D Eagle jet aircraft—named *Glamorous Glennis III*—and flew the plane past Mach 1 to commemorate the fiftieth anniversary of the historic X-1 mission. Then, fifteen years later, at the age of eighty-nine, he was copilot of another F-15 that broke the sound barrier to mark the sixty-fifth anniversary of that first sonic boom.

With Yeager's bigger-than-life persona, his heroic accomplishments and contributions to aviation, and his omnipresence in the media, it may be surprising to some that this is not at all the full story of this remarkable man and his contributions to his country. The often-overlooked truth is that Chuck Yeager was a bona fide hero years before he dropped loose from beneath that bomber for the historic but risky flight over the California high desert, the achievement that catapulted him into a life of celebrity. No, by then he had already proved himself as few others had, excelling in one of World War II's most dangerous jobs, and in the process contributing mightily to the defeat of Germany.

And it all started one day when then Army Air Forces enlisted man and airplane mechanic Private Charles Elwood Yeager decided he was tired of having to pull kitchen detail and guard duty. The day he noticed that it was the pilots who always seemed to have the prettiest girls on their arms. That the guys the ladies preferred were the ones without grease beneath their fingernails.

With that realization, the die was cast. But there were obstacles to overcome. Pilots had to be officers. He was an enlisted man. Most of them had college degrees. He was only a high school graduate. Then he happened to notice a posting on a bulletin board in the base mess hall.

And the often-overlooked early chapters of Chuck Yeager's heroic life and career were about to be written.

ONE

SKINNING SQUIRRELS IN HAMLIN

I was probably the last guy who will get to do the kind of flying I did. I came into the military as an 18-year-old kid before World War II, never having been in an airplane, never having even seen one on the ground. It turned into quite an opportunity.

—Chuck Yeager in 2002, after once again breaking the sound barrier as a pilot, this time in an F-15 Eagle, at the age of seventy-nine (quoted in the *Washington Post*)

Should someone drive into the little Appalachian Mountains town of Hamlin, West Virginia, from the northeast, he or she may not even notice when Highway 3 becomes Court Avenue just after crossing the Mud River and before passing the Carnivore BBQ restaurant. Then, only a few blocks before making a hard left turn at the Lincoln County Courthouse, the street runs directly in front of Hamlin PK-8 School. A quick glance toward the school reveals an unexpected roadside attraction, one interesting enough to merit a stop. It is a surprisingly impressive statue rising from a grassy area in front of the building. A statue that depicts a stocky man dressed in a flight suit, carrying an airplane pilot's helmet and gear, apparently gazing at something of interest in the sky just above the attorney's office across the street. An inscription on the statue's eight-foot-high pedestal informs us that this is a rendering of Brigadier General Charles E. "Chuck" Yeager, a native of this burg in the West Virginia mountains and clearly someone of whom the residents are immensely proud.

Even so, the statue was not erected until 1987, a full forty years after Yeager became the first man to break through the speed-of-sound barrier, the primary reason for his international fame. He is shown as he might have appeared forty years earlier, the day of the historic, record-breaking flight, but while the inscription concludes by noting that signal accomplishment, it also mentions his notable service to his country during World War II.

Yeager was born on February 13, 1923, several miles south of Hamlin, down the Mud River, in the tiny community of Myra. He was the second of five children for Albert Hal and Susie Mae Sizemore Yeager. The "Roaring Twenties" were little more than a whisper in rural West Virginia. Coal mining, logging, and dirt farming provided what little employment there was. Lincoln County was one of the most economically depressed areas in the nation even as much of America was booming during that decade. Although Yeager would later say his family never really thought of themselves as being poor, they would certainly have fallen into that category by any measure or definition. Typically, when everyone else in the area is going through the same experience, few are aware of their economic situation. Yeager would later note, "We had no choice. We just did what we had to do to get by." That was a philosophy that would stand him in good stead for the rest of his days.

As a boy, he and his brothers, Roy and Hal Jr., would spend hours roaming the woods on the family farm, learning to hunt and fish—for fun as well as for food—and developing a true appreciation for nature. They spent much of their time with their grandfather, who shared with them his knowledge of how to live off the land. Only later would Chuck learn that his family name had been converted from the German word *Jäger*, which means hunter, or fighter.

Tragedy struck the Yeager family three days before Christmas Day, 1930. Chuck and his older brother, Roy—Chuck was four and Roy was six—were playing with their dad's gun. Roy found some shells for the weapon and managed to load it. It accidentally fired, striking and killing their two-year-old sister, Doris Ann. She was buried in Lincoln Memorial Cemetery in Hamlin, two blocks from where her brother's statue would be erected over half a century later.

Contrary to what many might believe, the terrible accident did not lead to Hal Yeager hiding his weapons or forbidding his boys from ever touching them. Instead, he took blame for not already having taught them respect for guns of all kinds and how to properly use them. After all, they were an important and omnipresent part of the culture and were necessary in daily life, including putting food on the table. As Chuck would later say of the death of his baby sister, "There's nothing that you can do about it except learn." That, too, would remain his philosophy through many other trying situations.

It must have felt like a major boost to the family's fortunes when Hal Sr. left farming and mining behind and got a job working in the natural gas wells that blossomed on the surface ground above the coalfields. He soon moved the family from Myra—Yeager later described that town as little more than a post office and a couple of houses—to Hamlin, then a "big city" of four hundred souls. However, with his father often gone from home for days at a time as a requirement of his new job—he traveled with his drilling equipment all over West Virginia and Kentucky—and with the income only slightly elevated, it became even more imperative that Chuck and his brothers bring home game for food for his mother and their remaining younger sister, Pansy Lee. Also, the Great Depression would soon have far more effect on Appalachia and the Yeager family than the Roaring Twenties ever did.

The move upriver to Hamlin came when Chuck was five. It was not long before he was in school, a segue not altogether pleasing to a boy who preferred the outdoors, hunting, shooting, and skinning squirrels and rabbits. By the time he was seven, he regularly grabbed his .22 rifle, slipped out of his house early in the morning, shot squirrels, and then brought them home. Before heading to school, he would skin them and leave them in a pail of water for his mother to batter and fry up for supper. It was a far better meal than their usual mush, or cornbread crumbled into a bowl of buttermilk.

Initially, school came easy for young Chuck. He did so well in his studies that he skipped second grade and went right into third. Then things got tougher. He spent two years in fifth grade.

By high school, Chuck was an average and typically uninterested student except for those few classes in which he seemed remarkably well suited. Those included math—and especially geometry—and anything in which he could use his hands or that made practical sense to the boy. Touch-typing came easy for him, demonstrating manual dexterity. He could soon type more than sixty words per minute. But perhaps the education on which he would most rely in life came outside the classroom. That was from watching and helping his father—an accomplished, self-taught mechanic—as he operated and repaired the machinery associated with his new trade. The boy had shown early that he had a knack for understanding how the complicated equipment functioned and how to fix it if it broke. That included operating high-pressure-gas equipment and handling explosives.

As Chuck grew older, he spent much of his spare time working on his father's trucks, as well as the vehicles of other family members and friends. If he was not in school or hunting or fishing, he was overhauling someone's car or truck engine or helping his father keep his apparatus in service. It was a good thing young Chuck had such an interest. The family could not afford for any of the apparatus or vehicles to be out of service.

But it was not all work. He and his friends loved to play in the woods, building forts and fighting "wars." Those fun times also solidified the survival skills Chuck had picked up from his father and grandfather. He was at home in the thickets. And he loved being there.

Then, as a teenager, he showed exceptional athletic ability, playing both football and basketball at Hamlin High School. He also discovered he had been blessed with extraordinary eyesight. When he scoured the woods with friends or older men, he was able to see a deer in the brush long before anyone else spotted the animal. And his aim was superior: young Chuck almost always bagged whatever it was that he was shooting at.

When he graduated high school in June of 1941, there was no discussion about going to college. That was rarely an option for young people from that area. Yeager would later say that he was educated most by his parents and grandparents. They were honest and hardworking, but they were also blessed with country wisdom and common sense. They dutifully passed all that along to him and his siblings. And so did other elderly people in the community; Chuck enjoyed hanging around old people because, he would later say, "they were interesting and had a lot of tales to tell." Now, with the high school diploma stashed in a drawer somewhere, he figured he would continue to find work using his hands and mechanical skills, maybe in an auto shop somewhere. Or he would keep on helping his dad in the gas fields and maybe cobble a career out of that.

The boy who would one day become a legendary aviator had no thoughts whatsoever of entering that field. Growing up, he had no association with aircraft, other than occasionally hearing one drone along high overhead, likely a passenger plane bound for Charleston or Cincinnati. He hardly bothered to look up from the motor or pump he was working on or the mountain trail he was navigating at the time.

Then, one day when he was fifteen, someone came into the pool hall where Chuck had one of his several odd jobs. There he earned ten bucks a month racking the billiard balls for players.

The man shared the hot news that an airplane had just crashed nearby, on the bank of the Mud River. Curious, Chuck grabbed his bike and rode out to take a look. Sure enough, a Beechcraft plane had bellied in hard, coming to rest in a cornfield. The pilot had survived and walked away, and the aircraft was mostly intact. But the boy only took a quick look at the scene, climbed back onto his bike, and then pedaled away to take care of some chores. Being up close to an airplane held little to no interest for him.

He had not really considered military service, either. During his senior year of high school, while he was playing football and basketball and "chasing gals," war had broken out in Europe and tensions were running high between the United States and Japan. The American military had begun mobilizing already, just in case the United States was drawn into the conflict. That meant recruitment had been stepped up considerably. Yeager remembers that most boys he knew were suddenly becoming interested in the service. Many had already signed up. But the military still held little interest for him as he completed high school and went to work.

By the time the summer of 1941 was drawing to a close, and still with no firm plans for his future, Chuck got word that an Army recruiter and representatives of other service branches had set up shop for a few days right there in Hamlin. They were looking for enlistees from among the men who might have grown tired of the hard work and many hazards of the coal mines or lumberjacking. There continued to be talk of possible war, both in Europe and the Pacific—even murmurings about how deep the recently initiated draft of military-aged men might go to prepare for such an eventuality and how conscription might affect the labor force in the mines. Starting in November of 1940, all men aged twenty-one to thirty-five had been required to register and be available for service if called. That made it the first peacetime draft in US history. But such rumors and eventualities meant little to the folks who lived and worked in the mountains. Germany, Italy, and Japan might just as well have been on different planets from West Virginia.

However, something about serving in the military suddenly struck a chord with Yeager. It was not necessarily patriotism or defending his country. As a free spirit, he certainly was not attracted by the uniformity and regimentation of the service. It was more the thought that signing up would allow him to go off somewhere new and experience a bit more of the wide, wide world beyond the crest of the next ridge. That was something he had been thinking about lately: the world outside Lincoln County and West Virginia. Mostly on a whim, he grabbed his birth certificate—to prove he was eighteen years old—and his high school diploma and went down to at least have a talk with the recruiters.

When Yeager got there, he learned the Army recruiter was more specifically representing the Army Air Corps. And that they were especially in need of aircraft mechanics. The savvy recruiter knew he was fishing in teeming waters. Most every kid in these mountains was also a shade tree mechanic, accustomed to working on the vehicles of family and friends. (Note that the aviation branch of the US Army was called the Army Air Corps until June of 1941, when it would be renamed the Army Air Forces. It was the predecessor of what would become another independent service branch, the US Air Force, gaining equal standing alongside the Army, Navy, Marines, Coast Guard, and, much later, the Space Force. That major change to becoming a full, independent service branch would occur in 1947, which just happened to be a significant year in the career of Chuck Yeager, too.)

The young man was immediately hooked on what the recruiter told him. Learning about airplane engines sounded like a fine way to become an even better mechanic, to find some excitement somewhere else besides the shadowy hollers and rushing streams of his home, and to finally get to see considerably more of the world. Since he was now eighteen, he could sign up on his own, without the signature of a parent. And that was exactly what he did.

He would later say, "I guess the Army recruiter was better than the guy from the Navy." Yeager would also admit he was influenced by another local boy who had gone away to pilot training and came back home on leave gushing about all the excitement and fun he was experiencing. Even so, Chuck still had no thoughts of flying. He was just ready for a change of scenery and more training as a mechanic that might enable him to make a living when his time in the service was up.

Chuck's dad had little to say about his boy's enlistment. As Yeager later wrote, his father's only advice while growing up was to never buy a vehicle not manufactured by General Motors. And then, the day his boy enlisted in the Army Air Corps, his father's lone admonition was "Don't ever gamble."

A young man who had rarely ventured outside the confines of the heavily forested Appalachian Mountains, who had only seen an airplane up close when that one crashed into the corn-field over by the river, and who had little idea of the politics surrounding the growing flames of war that would soon con-sume the whole world was about to embark on a radical new course in his life.

Even so, Chuck Yeager had no idea that, by signing those enlistment papers that day in September of 1941, he was about to go off across the country to strange territory and, once there, would soon be doing exactly what he had been placed on this planet to do.

And that was not working as an airplane mechanic.

TWO

FLYING SERGEANT

A big part of it is being at the right place at the right time.
You either are or you aren't. You don't have to be good to be
a legend. All you have to do is live. That's about the way it
stacks up.

—Chuck Yeager on the CBS television show
Sunday Morning, October 23, 1983

War leads to more technical innovation than just about any other human activity. When faced with conquer-or-be-conquered, the military, scientists, engineers, laborers, industrialists, and others crank up the research as well as the means of production to get the upper hand against the enemy. That certainly applied to aircraft just before and during the early stages of World War II.

With Hitler's Luftwaffe blasting the way for the German march across Europe, Great Britain knew they needed to prepare, not only to deflect the inevitable air attacks over the British Isles, but to also send their own Royal Air Force bombers on offensive missions over the Continent to try to slow down the Nazi advance. Prevailing thought before the war began was that closely packed formations of bombers could protect themselves, even when conducting daylight runs, using their own armament. That soon proved to be incorrect, confirmed tragically once the shooting started when Great Britain declared war against Germany on September 3, 1939. Some sort of high-speed, maneuverable fighter plane, one that could match the range of British bombers and help shield them from enemy fighters, would be the best possible solution. But at the time such a craft was thought to be an engineering and practical impossibility.

Wartime innovation sprang up to fill the need. It was in April of 1940, prior to the United States entering the war and just as young Chuck Yeager was completing his junior year of high school there in Hamlin, that the British approached American company North American Aviation with a request: they wanted NAA to modify the existing Curtiss P-40 fighter to meet the requirements for a suitable bomber escort plane. At the time, NAA had a license from Curtiss to produce the aircraft. The idea was to use the planes for two purposes: primarily to fend off any bombers that might cross the English Channel and attack British soil, but also to shield RAF bombers on runs over occupied Europe and, hopefully one day, Germany. North American countered with a different idea. Rather than use the airframe of somebody else's product, they proposed building from scratch a more modern plane, one that would have other uses in addition to air-to-air combat. From the day the contract was executed, it took only a little over one hundred days before the first experimental airframe rolled off an assembly line. A test pilot successfully flew the first one—by then dubbed the P-51 "Mustang"—in October of 1940.

Even with that impressive developmental record, the new craft came just a bit late. On September 7, 1940, three hundred Luftwaffe bombers rumbled in over the English Channel and began blasting London, unleashing over 330 tons of ordnance. It was the beginning of the "blitzkrieg," and the vicious bombings would take place for fifty-seven consecutive days, then continue on most nights until May of 1941.

That was just as Chuck Yeager was accepting his high school diploma back in Hamlin, West Virginia, earning spending money racking billiard balls, working on neighbors' cars, and helping his father in the gas fields.

Adolf Hitler's plan was to keep Britain at bay, neutralized, and sap the British of their will to fight while he marched eastward with the intent of invading and conquering Russia. Then, when that mission was accomplished, he would pivot westward and easily claim a depleted England. America was a minor factor. The United States seemed so averse to entering another foreign war—one not directly threatening its shores—that they would remain on the sidelines until it was too late, and the Third Reich would soon become a true European empire.

Once fully tested, the Mustang fighter turned out to be very well suited for air-to-air skirmishes. And with continued modifications, along with a major change in approach toward the protection necessary for bombers over enemy territory, the plane was exactly what was needed for that specialized escort duty as well. The Mustang's wings and fuselage were of a new design that resulted in more speed and maneuverability than its predecessors. Aluminum was used everywhere feasible, making the plane much lighter, thus requiring less fuel. From the start, being able to carry more gas and allowing for a longer range was a key goal. The engine cooling system developed for the Mustang was radically different and worked well (although it later proved vulnerable to damage from opposing fighters' bullets). But perhaps the most important part of the plan was that the airplane was designed to be built quickly and efficiently on only slightly modified but already existing assembly lines. And it could be accomplished at a bargain-basement cost of about $40,000 per unit.

The P-51 Mustang was not only a winner but a perfect example of necessity being the mother of invention.

The British had initially ordered 320 planes, even though they were not convinced that such a warbird was even feasible when the original contract was signed. They were desperate for something to help the cause against the Germans. Once they saw how well the Mustang performed during tests in September 1940, they promptly placed an order for 300 more. The workers at North American Aviation then had to scramble to build them and deliver them on schedule. And in one of the truly heroic efforts of World War II, they did exactly that.

Once the P-51 was in use—by both British and American pilots, since the United States was forced to enter the war after the Japanese attack on Pearl Harbor in December of 1941—worrisome limitations of the hastily designed plane cropped up. The biggest problem was that the strong, reliable Allison engine initially used in the Mustang lost considerable power once the plane was operating at an altitude higher than about 15,000 feet. Most plane-to-plane fighting over Europe took place at heights greater than that. That issue also made it difficult for the early models serving as escorts for bomber squadrons. Best practice was for the escort aircraft to fly several thousand feet above the high-flying bombers, watching for enemy attack planes, then swoop down and try to surprise and deflect the aggressors. A switch to an engine manufactured by Rolls-Royce greatly improved the plane's high-altitude power and speed.

By the time Chuck Yeager was so effectively piloting a Mustang, they were also being fitted with special disposable 108-gallon fuel tanks attached to each wing that greatly extended the aircraft's range. Previously, the plane's only gas tank was located in the fuselage, directly behind the pilot and cockpit. It held 85 gallons. Once the aircraft had used up all the fuel from those add-on tanks or if the pilot simply wanted more maneuverability, the wing tanks could be jettisoned, making them lighter and giving them significantly more speed and flexibility.

This innovation gave the aircraft enough range—approaching 2,000 miles—so they could accompany bombers from Great Britain, across and deep into Europe, including over Germany, and then have enough fuel left to return to base. And the P-51 pilots could also do considerable dogfighting along the way before having to worry so much about running out of fuel. German fighters were near equal to the Mustangs in most respects but they would never achieve the kind of range the P-51s had.

The Mustang proved especially suited for a brutal but beautiful type of one-on-one aerial warfare. The first use of the term "dogfight" appears to have been in an article in the British newspaper the *Graphic* in May 1918 reporting on the death of World War I German fighter ace Baron Manfred von Richthofen. Although the dashing airman was by far the most famous fighter pilot of the time, the first actual plane-to-plane combat had occurred before the war, on November 30, 1913. That came during the Mexican Revolution. In that melee, two American mercenary pilots, each fighting on behalf of opposing forces, fired pistols at each other in midair until they ran out of bullets. At that point they shook their fists and flew away. Pilots have engaged in dogfights, with gradually improving and more effective ordnance and tactics, ever since. And all along, in a precedent set by Baron von Richthofen—who was credited with eighty combat kills—the pilots involved in those daring skirmishes in the sky have acquired something of a romanticized aura.

Not long after the Mustang's introduction into World War II, the Germans realized that they had no definitive answer for the P-51 fighters. Their Messerschmitt aircraft lacked the speed to effectively dogfight with the Mustangs. Even so, such combat could be deadly for pilots on both sides. Many planes and pilots were lost. Later, as tactics developed to meet reality rather than theory, American pilots were told to no longer spend their entire runs shielding the bombers but to go in search of the enemy aircraft anywhere they could find them. That included strafing planes that were still parked on the ground. The approach worked well and made the P-51 Mustang especially effective in shutting down the Luftwaffe.

By the middle of 1944, the threat to Allied bombing missions was greatly diminished (though still very much present), thanks in great part to the P-51. Daytime bombing runs could be resumed, keeping constant pressure on the Germans from the air. Because of the early decision to make the Mustang easy and quick to build, their sheer numbers in the skies over Europe offered a major advantage. As had the Japanese, the Germans had greatly underestimated the industrial capacity and the sheer will of Americans to prosecute the war once they were dragged into it by the attack on Pearl Harbor.

By May of 1945, Army Air Forces units claimed they had shot down almost 5,000 enemy aircraft. That was about half of all the planes blasted from the sky by the Allies in the European theater. Add to that the more than 4,000 enemy aircraft claimed to have been destroyed while they were still on the ground. In the process of inflicting all that damage, the Army Air Forces lost about 2,500 aircraft.

Although the Mustang and its remarkable capabilities were perfectly suited for the job, the success of the Allies must also be attributed to the men who designed, built, serviced, and flew those birds. The skill, dedication, and bravery of the pilots of that remarkable warplane arguably contributed the most to its success. Many gave their lives in the process. But as with other means of fighting a war, having warriors especially adept at what they did—the right people doing the right job using the right equipment—helped secure the victory against a worthy and highly motivated adversary.

Hermann Göring, the commander of the Luftwaffe and a

World War I fighter pilot himself, was quoted as saying, "When I saw Mustangs over Berlin, I knew the jig was up." It was the right equipment for the job. And the Army Air Forces found the right people to make use of it.

When Charles E. Yeager signed on the dotted line committing to that two-year hitch in the Air Corps in September of 1941, he likely had never even heard of a Mustang. And certainly not the aircraft that bore the name. As he packed his bag and prepared to head off for training, he surely never considered the possibility of being in a cockpit of a fighter plane in the middle of a dogfight. Or even of firing a gun at anything other than a deer or rabbit. He may or may not have been aware that he would not be eligible for flight training in the Air Corps— even if he had been interested in such a thing—because of his background and lack of college credits.

Young Chuck was certainly patriotic. His family had instilled in him a love for the United States and all it stood for. He also had a strong sense of duty. Neither of those played much of a role in the decision he made to join the service, though.

When he rode that train across the country as a newly enlisted private, the only thing on his mind was learning how to work on and repair those airplane engines. And to take in all the scenery and atmosphere he could. Then, when he arrived at Victorville Army Air Field, California, he discovered that the place where he would undergo that training and soak up some new atmosphere looked more like a moonscape than it did a military facility. Where was the ocean? The trees? The mountains? The bright lights of Hollywood?

Victorville Army Air Field was located in the midst of the

Mojave Desert near Victorville, California. Some of town's leading citizens had approached the Army with the idea of constructing a training base for pilots near their city. They proudly pointed out that the area offered clear, dry air with more than 360 days a year of rainless weather. There were miles and miles of flat ground in all directions. The perfect setting for flying and testing airplanes. Plus, the area offered all the amenities of Victorville, a town located along the legendary Route 66, and its population of about 50,000 welcoming people. A town big enough to offer all amenities without the distractions and security headaches of a bigger or more glamorous city.

The Army, already occupied by thoughts of potential war, agreed it was a fine place for such a training facility. Construction commenced in July of 1941 and was finally being completed when Private Yeager showed up for duty, stepping off the train into the middle of a dust storm.

The first class for pilots and bombardiers was not scheduled to begin at Victorville until February of 1942, but the Army would require a ready fleet of aircraft and a well-trained ground crew to service the planes before that training could begin. That included competent mechanics, ready and in place. Yeager was perfectly fine with being one of those ground crewmen.

He was also pleasantly surprised when he learned the engines and other equipment on the airplanes were so easy for him to understand and work on, not that different from the vehicles and pumping equipment back home on which he had cut his teeth. Even the other parts of the airplanes, from the airframes to the radios, were no challenge for the mechanically inclined young man. Before long, Yeager had advanced to crew chief on the AT-11 Kansan aircraft and was assigned to teach others how to keep the bird flying for each crop of new pilots. The newcomers were perfectly capable of crashing their trainers on their own. They needed no help from malfunctioning engines or other systems.

The Army Air Forces AT-11 was an advanced twin-engine trainer manufactured by Beech Aircraft. It was primarily used for instructing bombardiers, gunners, navigators, and pilots prior to and during World War II. Estimates are that better than 90 percent of all bombardiers who saw duty in the war trained in this model aircraft. The plane was constructed to look remarkably like the B-17 Flying Fortress or the B-24 Liberator bombers. They typically carried ten practice bombs on each training flight, dropping them on sandy targets and unwary critters out there in the California high desert.

From the beginning, Chuck Yeager was well pleased with his duty and the training he was receiving. He was less thrilled with the opportunities for social life or fun out there in the middle of the Mojave. Specifically, there were not many unattached females out there, and the dashing pilot trainees had dibs on what few there were.

Before long, Yeager became convinced that he knew just about all there was to know about the AT-11 Kansan's Pratt & Whitney engines and its other parts. Also, an additional aspect of his duty required that he work in the base kitchen and mess hall, serving up SOS—"shit on a shingle"—and washing dishes. And that he regularly stand guard duty at the gates that provided entry into the base, protecting everyone stationed there from an invasion by gopher rats, rattlesnakes, and Japanese spies. He was more than ready to defend his country by doing something more interesting and challenging. And preferably somewhere else, at some spot where he might occasionally see a tree or a squirrel. Or a girl.

Then one day the private happened to pass a bulletin board in the mess hall. His sharp eye caught a new posting thumbtacked there. Something made him stop and read it. That quick glance and pause would redirect Chuck Yeager's life in a major and historic way.

With the war now underway, the Army Air Forces were looking for men interested in becoming pilots. That, according to the bulletin board notice, now included enlisted men, like Chuck Yeager. Even those with no college credit or previous flying experience. Candidates would face considerably relaxed qualifications for pilot training, although the announcement promised that it would still be difficult for many to meet the criteria no matter how desperate the Army was for flyboys. More than half of all applicants would fail the physical examination.

The "flying sergeants" program promised, though, that even someone with a rank of private and with nothing more than a high school diploma could apply for pilot training. And even better, anyone who successfully completed his pilot training would emerge from the program with the rank of sergeant. Although originally created in 1912, the program had been mostly dormant until the demands of a two-pronged war on opposite sides of the planet dramatically ramped up the requirement for pilots. And by the time the first recruits were flying World War II combat missions, the average age of the newcomers was eighteen to twenty years old, much younger than previous pilots, who required a college degree to qualify for training.

Before enlisting in the Army and coming to Victorville, Chuck Yeager had never flown in an airplane before. Never even been close to one except for the Beech he had briefly observed stuck in the muddy cornfield back in Hamlin. After arriving in Victorville, the first and only opportunity he had to go up in the air did not turn out well at all. When a maintenance officer asked him to ride along while he checked out one of the AT-11s Yeager had just serviced, things deteriorated immediately after takeoff. As the pilot banked, climbed, and dived, doing touch-and-go landings in dry lake beds, testing the recent repairs, the young mechanic turned green in the face and became violently airsick. Yeager promptly vomited all over the cockpit. And once the pilot set the AT-11 back down and taxied to the hangar, Yeager climbed from the plane and staggered away, vowing never to leave the ground again.

What was it Grandpa Yeager always said about flying in an airplane or becoming a coal miner? "Thank you, no. I don't plan on ever gettin' any lower than diggin' taters or higher than pullin' corn!"

But the powerful lure of doing something new, of seeking greater excitement, quickly overcame Chuck Yeager's reluctance. He located the right guy with the right form to complete and submitted his request to undergo training to become a "flying sergeant."

Then he pretty much forgot about it.

But to his considerable surprise, he was eventually accepted.

Conditionally, of course. He would have to pass the physical and then show that he could master in the classroom as well as in the air all the complexities of aeronautical physics.

And, of course, demonstrate that he could climb, bank, and dive an airplane without losing his lunch.

THREE

FLYING BECOMES FUN

I was in maintenance, saw pilots had beautiful girls on their arms, didn't have dirty hands, so I applied.
—Chuck Yeager, circa 2016, when asked why he decided to become a pilot

Chuck Yeager was very fortunate to have been blessed at birth with exceptional eyesight. According to local lore around Hamlin, he once spied and killed a deer at six hundred yards. Nobody else in his group had even seen the animal and wondered at the time what he was shooting at. His physical examination for the flying sergeants program, which included his first professional eye test, ultimately confirmed the gift. His vision was measured at 20/10. And he easily met the other physical requirements for entry into the elite program. That examination was performed on December 4, 1941, only three days before the Japanese attack on Pearl Harbor. Then, with the war viciously underway for America and ramping up rapidly, Yeager could only cool his heels and continue to work on AT-11s, keeping them flying for trainees, schooling other mechanics, and doing his part while he awaited acceptance and orders to go learn to fly and fight for his country.

Those orders would not come through until a full six months later. Then he would spend another six months attending various preflight training schools. He would not fly again during that time, but he did worry about whether or not he could overcome his airsickness based on that one uncomfortable experience in the AT-11.

His initial flight training took place in Hemet, California, eighty miles south of Victorville and on the other side of the San Bernardino Mountains from where he had spent the war so far. Next was basic pilot training, Yeager's introduction to the Vultee BT-13 Valiant single-engine plane at Taft, California, near Bakersfield. That would be the former mechanic's first opportunity to climb into the pilot's seat of an airplane for a purpose other than repairing something that was busted.

But once Yeager was assigned to the next level of pilot training—at Luke Field in Arizona in February of 1943—he had another concern about his potential for success as an airplane driver. He realized that he was still one of the few enlisted men in Class 43C. Attrition had already taken its toll on the enlisted men who yearned to be pilots. Almost all the others in his class were college men, ready to accept appointment as commissioned officers once they earned their wings. He was aware, too, that the other trainees were several years older than he was and that they looked down with considerable scorn on their younger and less educated classmates. Some were even West Point grads.

Still less than two years out of high school and away from the West Virginia mountains, Yeager would later admit that he was somewhat intimidated by those guys and wondered if he could keep up and compete with them. It would be one of the few instances in his life that he would have doubts about what he could accomplish. He would soon learn, however, that once they climbed into a trainer and left the end of the runway behind, their backgrounds mattered little.

He quickly put his other big worry out of the way, too. He still got woozy on his first few training flights at Taft but soon the airsickness waned. He never once threw up on his ride-along flight instructor. And with his natural athletic ability and God-given physical coordination, Yeager quickly realized that simultaneously handling the trainer aircraft's stick and rudder came easy for him. Every move and action in the cockpit simply made sense to him. Not so much so for many of his older and better-educated classmates.

Luke Field—deactivated in 1946, reactivated as Luke Air Force Base in 1951, and still a major training site for pilots—was located about fifteen miles west of Phoenix, which was hardly a bustling metropolis at the time. As with Victorville, the town of Phoenix had lobbied the Army Air Corps to construct an air base there on desert scrub land owned by the city. They offered to lease almost 1,500 acres to the government for a fee of one dollar per year. The deal was done, and the first class of would-be Army Air Corps pilots—renamed days later as "Army Air Forces"—began training there on June 6, 1941, almost six months to the day before Pearl Harbor and America's entry into World War II. That first class would graduate on August 15. However, with construction still underway on the facility, they had to do all their flying out of Sky Harbor Airport in Phoenix.

The base's name was late in coming, too. The original Luke Field, named for World War I Medal of Honor pilot Second

Lieutenant Frank Luke Jr., a native of Phoenix, was located at that time at Pearl Harbor, Hawaii. That base agreed to give up its name to the Arizona location. Luke Field—the Arizona one—went on to train and graduate more than 12,000 aviators during World War II and was easily the Army Air Forces' largest base for preparing pilots during and after the war.

All the flight trainees soon became aware that the curriculum was being developed on the fly. Air-to-air combat and strategic bombing techniques were constantly changing, based on what was happening in the real world and the new equipment becoming available for aviators. In World War I, pilots were flying planes that could barely exceed 100 miles per hour. They typically had open cockpits, so nobody could fly very high. In combat, the object was to try to shoot the pilot and kill him with their small-caliber guns or hope for some damage if a stray bullet hit the motor or accidentally cut a wire or cord somewhere. Otherwise, their bullets went right through the fabric skin and did no damage bad enough to eliminate the foe from the fight.

Now, with Allied fighter planes capable of 300 to 400 miles per hour, equipped with sealed cockpits and oxygen—and soon gravity suits so the pilots could survive while climbing higher, diving faster, and making turns that created huge g-forces—they could use a lot more of the sky as a battlefield.

The new equipment required a much different skill set for fliers, too. Quicker reflexes. Better eyesight. Instinctive maneuverability. An understanding of aeronautics, physics, and mechanics. The tenacity to follow an enemy plane all the way until it hit the ground and could be confirmed as a "kill." If the trainee did not already possess those capabilities and qualities, he had to learn the ones he could and compensate for the ones he did not. Otherwise, he might well not survive the training, much less actual combat. It had become obvious that the enemy had well-trained pilots and more-than-adequate fighter aircraft, plus—at least in Europe—the advantage of doing most of the fighting over their home or occupied territory. The reality of the war that was being fought had a direct impact on the pilot training that Yeager was getting.

For him, the flying part came easy. Rarely lacking self-confidence—and having overcome his feelings of inadequacy over his classmates—he was only moderately surprised to find that he was a stone-cold natural airplane pilot. He felt as if the plane's controls were nothing more than an extension of his own body.

However, he would later be quoted as saying that there was no such thing as a "natural" pilot. He came to believe that in any comparison the man with the greatest amount of experience was almost always the better flyer. But even then he readily acknowledged that he possessed the physical makeup necessary to excel. But it came only with plenty of hard work and practice. He developed those skills to the utmost, starting out there in the San Joaquin Valley and continuing in the sweltering Arizona desert.

Natural or not, his first solo flight in the BT-13 at Taft left him nervous beforehand and then spent and sweating once he was back on the runway. It was not long, though, before he felt as comfortable in the trainer—all by himself—as he had back home, piloting any of the old cars he fixed up and brought back to life to go out in search of fun and girls.

It was the classroom and the physical aspects of the curriculum at all three stops that proved to be a daunting challenge for him. Washing out and going back to being a mechanic was a distinct possibility all along the way. The flying part was easy and fun, and he was good at it. The classroom and physical training parts were hell and almost ended his piloting plans.

The Army was aware they were training these young men for tough duty against a well-prepared foe who employed effective equipment. By design, the program was intensely competitive. High attrition was the result. That was also by design. The Army Air Forces wanted only the best. That included many steps along the way, beginning with the physical exam, which weeded out fully half of the men initially accepted into the program. Then only about half those who got through that gauntlet and moved on would successfully complete the two months of instruction and receive their pilot's wings. Although numbers are not available, many failed to complete the program because they were killed. More than a few of the Luke Field trainees crashed their trainers and did not survive.

Yeager and his class trained six days a week for just over two months. When they were not in their bunks, they were either in the air or in the classroom. Sundays were not off days, though. The trainees were out on the drill field, learning to march in formation, a skill few of the men felt they would ever require in the future. The Army begged to differ.

It was good luck that Yeager's tenure there in the Arizona

desert came in February and March of 1943, in the relatively mild winter, instead of during the area's notoriously brutal summer. The first classes at Luke encountered temperatures well above 100 degrees. It was even hotter on the flight line. That extreme heat also caused issues in the air, creating turbulence and stressing airplane engines, not to mention pilot durability.

But even in the relatively cool months, Yeager and the others were subject to plenty of PT, physical training. Without enough trainer aircraft to go around, the men had to spend a lot of time waiting for their turns to go fly. The instructors took advantage of that downtime to have their trainees do calisthenics. Seemingly endless push-ups, leg lifts, and jumping jacks. The reasoning was that the duty for which they were bound required exceptional physical fitness. But the trainees soon realized it was all a part of the plan to try to wash out those who were not totally dedicated to becoming pilots. Even though the need for pilots was great, the rationale was that the war required tough men to do a tough job. Those who could not endure PT in the Arizona sun would be no match for Japanese or German fighter pilots at 30,000 feet.

Chuck Yeager had immediately realized that he loved flying. Once sickened by dives and touch-and-go landings, he now found he enjoyed performing such maneuvers and would usually do so until he ran out of fuel or was scolded for not promptly returning to base. Piloting an airplane also brought out an inherent character trait. He thrived on competition and longed to show that he was the best at whatever he did, just as he had in sports back home. His cockiness led him to look for ways to dramatically demonstrate what he could do up there in the blue Arizona sky. He loved to dive close to other student pilots, plunging in from their blind sides and challenging them to mock dogfights. He could also line up on practice targets—in the air and on the ground—before most of the other trainees had even seen them, then dive on the objectives at impossibly daring angles and blistering speeds. The boldness and risk-taking by this "student" both frightened and amazed his classmates. It gave his instructors heartburn.

One of Yeager's favorite activities was buzzing structures, animals, highways, tractors in fields, and sometimes even people on the ground, diving in out of the blue, his engine screaming, giving the "target" a good dusting. He considered such hijinks to be good practice for what lay ahead. The Army felt it violated protocol, risking man and machine, and was, by the way, terrible PR.

The young pilot was called on the carpet and duly reprimanded—something that would happen repeatedly throughout Yeager's long career. He always apologized and promised it would not happen again. Then it would. In his mind, it was the best preparation he could ever get. And besides, it was a hell of a lot of fun.

Despite his penchant for mischief, Yeager's primary instructor was convinced that his student would make a fine fighter pilot. Early on, he had assumed Chuck had been a pilot before enlisting and had had plenty of hours at the stick prior to joining the Army. He was surprised to learn the young man with the difficult-to-understand drawl had only a few months' time in a pilot seat. So, when the time came, he recommended that

Yeager be awarded his wings, be certified for combat, and move on to the next phase of fighter training. As soon as graduation was completed, he was set to report to the 363rd Fighter Squadron (part of the 357th Fighter Group) and be promoted to the rank of sergeant in the Army Air Forces. The flak-filled skies over Europe would be his destination in only a few more months, after still more intensive and duty-specific preparation.

Graduation day was to be a big event for the Yeager family. Chuck's dad and younger brother, Hal Jr., made the long trek out to Arizona to attend the ceremony and see him receive his wings. But as the ceremony approached, Chuck had cause for worry. Rumors were that the Army was already making significant changes to the flying sergeant program. There were concerns about how this would affect his promotion to higher rank. Some still felt privates should not be able to become fighter pilots and be so readily promoted to sergeant.

He was also afraid that some of that flying fun he had been having, incidents serious enough to end up on his permanent military record, might now surface and keep him from graduating in good standing. All those times buzzing cows and mock dogfighting with reluctant classmates and instructors had resulted in some strong reprimands that might now come back to bite him.

And then there was the issue of the dead horse back in Victorville.

Yeager hated guard duty. That was a prime motivator for him to seek pilot training in the first place. Standing guard was boring, tedious, and seemingly never-ending, yet he had to take his turn, just like everybody else in the class. One night he decided to break the monotony by showing his fellow gate guard how well he could shoot with the .30-caliber machine gun they had at their disposal. He had seen some horses grazing nearby but intended to shoot at scrub brush much closer. Just raise some dust and panic some lizards. He fired off several rounds, shot higher than he intended to, because (he would later testify) the sight on the gun was not calibrated properly, and accidentally killed one of the horses. The farmer raised hell, the Army had to pay for the dead animal, and Yeager, by then a corporal, was court-martialed. The punishment ended up being relatively light, but the black mark on his service record could now, he feared, possibly prevent him from graduating from flight school and receiving whatever promotion in rank he was due.

For once, though, military red tape and bureaucracy were a big help to Yeager. The records, stacked in some office somewhere, backlogged due to the ramp-up for war, had not yet caught up to him.

The worrisome changes in the flying sergeant program proved to be positive for Yeager, too. Instead of being promoted to sergeant, enlisted men completing flight training would now become noncommissioned flight officers. He was advancing from the rank of corporal to flight officer. He likely did not think about it then, but that would put him in line to eventually become a brigadier general in the Air Force should he remain in the service long enough.

Although the official date of his promotion was March 9, it was on March 10, 1943—not quite a month after his twentieth birthday—that Charles Yeager graduated flight school and had the hard-won wings pinned onto his chest.

However, he was still not bound for the war. At least not yet. Now that he had been officially designated as a fighter pilot, he had to move on for still more advanced training. He headed five hundred miles north to the Tonopah Bombing and Gunnery Range, located in remote silver-mining country in Nevada, about halfway between Las Vegas and Reno. Legend has it that silver was discovered in the area when a prospector picked up a rock to hurl at his runaway mule and noticed his projectile had a certain glint to it. That set off a silver and gold rush that soon had the town booming, at least for a while. But since the 1940s the military facility there in Tonopah has provided most of the town's employment.

Tonopah presented new and more grueling challenges to Yeager and his fellow pilots. The attrition continued there, with many of them accidentally crashing their P-39 Airacobra training aircraft. Yeager, like many pilots, never used the word "crash." He preferred the more descriptive term, "auger in." In his memoir, he would later write that the young pilots killed at Tonopah would have certainly been the first to die in combat had they somehow survived their training. In addition, they would have also destroyed a better airplane than their trainer when they augered in over there in Europe or in the Pacific. He compared the manner in which many of them died to some dumb hillbilly doing something stupid and driving a Cadillac off a bridge. He made it a point to avoid being around those he considered inferior, careless, or dangerous pilots, afraid it might rub off on him like a fungus.

Probably as a defense tactic, Yeager developed a shockingly callous attitude about the loss of life that continually occurred all around them out there in the Mojave Desert. "When one of them became a grease spot on the tarmac, I almost felt relieved," he later wrote. "It was better to bury a weak sister in training than in combat, where he might not only bust his ass but do something that would bust two or three asses in addition to his own."

Even with that, he admitted mostly just getting mad at those who died for doing something so senseless and while still so young. The loss of life at Tonopah turned out to be excessive, even for the Army Air Forces' almost Darwinian weeding-out process. Due to the carnage, the group commander was relieved of duty while Yeager was still stationed there.

Yeager and his buddies found several ways to deal with the loss of life among their fellow trainee fighter pilots as well as the brutal training regimen they were undergoing. They went out every chance they had to blow off steam and get rip-roaring drunk. They also spent time in the local casinos playing blackjack—despite Yeager's father's admonition never to gamble—or frequenting one of the several houses of prostitution that operated in the area. On a rare day off, Yeager and a friend, a Texan with a similar love of the outdoors, would often borrow a jeep. Then they sped out into the desert, shooting jackrabbits, flattening cacti, and careening up and down the canyons all day. They were the same canyons the pilots buzzed and strafed each day and they enjoyed seeing—at ground level—the results of their gun and bombing practice.

Yeager and others believed the aircraft being used to train the new fighter pilots were a contributing cause of some of the fatal crashes. The Bell P-39 Airacobra was America's primary fighter plane when the war first began, but it was something of an odd duck. The engine was placed behind the pilot in the middle of the plane's fuselage. The single propeller was driven by a long shaft that ran from the engine through the cockpit. A 37mm cannon barrel stuck out from the center of the prop. The placement of the three landing gears most resembled a tricycle's wheels and made landings tricky.

Although the P-39 was the best fighter the US had going into the war, it certainly had issues. If a pilot stalled the plane, it tended to go into a roll, like a spinning top, and it was difficult to get it back under control before it bored a hole into the desert sand. That made it difficult for the pilot to bail out, too. So did the plane's cockpit entry and exit, which Yeager described as looking like a car door.

While the P-39 had sufficient power and speed for air-to-air combat at low altitudes, its small wings made it unsuitable for use up high where the air was thin. And that was where most of the action in Europe was taking place. That was the primary reason the Royal Air Force rejected the plane, even as desperate as they were for more aircraft. That led instead to the rapid and successful development of the P-51 Mustang. The United States began phasing out the P-39 over Europe as well once the superior P-51s began to come online and show their capabilities. However, the Soviet Union snatched up every P-39 they could get, since most of their plane-to-plane fighting was occurring at lower altitudes. Many Soviet pilots became "aces" in Airacobras. And the P-39 served the Allies well in the Pacific during island assaults.

Even with those problems, Chuck Yeager had no qualms at all about the Airacobra. While his contemporaries complained about the plane, Yeager informed them that he would gladly take the bird to war if given the chance. One of his squadron mates would later say, "Chuck became the yardstick by which we could measure the rest [of the pilots] as they joined us, several each month. Yeager could fly. Right from the start, he was pretty impressive."

One thing did bother Yeager. The P-39 required considerable maintenance, especially considering how much use they were getting. Ground crew personnel had become more and more scarce, with most of them needed at bases in England and all around the Pacific. And those men who were available were insufficiently trained. Chuck Yeager was often seen with the cowling raised, working on his own plane, just to lessen the odds of it breaking while he was practicing dogfighting, strafing, night landings, skip bombing, or dive-bombing.

After almost three months in Tonopah, Yeager was on the move again in late June of 1943. The next destination was Santa Rosa, California, in the wine country north of San Francisco Bay. The day his squad left Tonopah, the girls from the local cathouses showed up to give them a proper send-off, with hot coffee, sandwiches, and doughnuts. Everyone knew this next stop would put the young pilots—most of them still in their early twenties, like twenty-year-old Chuck Yeager—one step closer to combat.

But, for Chuck, there was about to be an unexpected but prophetic detour that placed him close to home for a short time, doing a job that would later make him internationally famous. Then, after rejoining his squadron, he would meet a person who would play a major role in his life. The person for whom most of the airplanes he would fly throughout the rest of his long career would be named.

FOUR

GLAMOROUS GLEN

It's your duty to fly the airplane. If you get killed in it, you don't know anything about it anyway. Duty is paramount. It's that simple if you're a military guy. You don't say "I'm not going to do that—that's dangerous." If it's your duty to do it, that's the way it is.

—Chuck Yeager, Academy of Achievement interview, January 14, 2019

Next on the training schedule for Chuck Yeager's squadron of eager fighter pilots was a short turn in Santa Rosa, California, learning the finer points of bomber escort duty and coastal patrolling. Then would come a "finishing school" at Oroville, California, about seventy miles north of Sacramento, at a former municipal airport leased by the Army and redesignated as Oroville Army Air Field. Yeager would also spend some time at Moffett Field at the southernmost end of San Francisco Bay, near Mountain View, California. There, his commanding officer was a fellow named Jimmy Stewart, the famous actor. Stewart would later fly bomber missions during the war, a period he would always describe as the most important and memorable time in his life.

However, when Chuck Yeager opened his travel orders before departing Tonopah, he discovered his course had been redirected and would be different from that of his fellow 357th Fighter Group pilots. And the Army had a good reason for excusing him from much of the training at Santa Rosa and Mountain View.

Because of his strong dual capabilities as both a maintenance mechanic and a fighter pilot, the Army wanted him to spend the next two months instead at Wright Field—now Wright-Patterson Air Force Base—in Dayton, Ohio. The man who would arguably become the most well-known test pilot in history one day was about to get an early taste of that job. It would be representative of what such duty involved but not necessarily as exciting or interesting as what he would one day gain fame for doing. Even so, he was surprised that he drew the assignment at all. Test pilots were almost all college graduates, usually with engineering degrees. But someone up the command chain was bright enough to know that this particular pilot was uniquely qualified for such work.

Yeager would be helping perfect a new propeller for the Bell P-39 Airacobra. He considered it easy duty. The assignment was to fly as much as he could in an airplane with which he was intimately familiar, make detailed observations of the performance of the new propeller, watch for any specific problems, and keep painstaking maintenance records on the airplane.

Easy but mostly boring. At least he got to spend a lot of time in the air, putting the plane through its paces. By this time Yeager preferred being in the sky, where there were no roads, no stop signs or speed limits, instead of remaining tethered to the ground. Plus he also had the opportunity during downtime to fly and become familiar with some other types of aircraft. On one of his first such flights, he took out a Republic P-47 Thunderbolt. At a weight of close to five tons, it was easily one of the heaviest fighters in the Army's arsenal. But it was also the favorite ride for many pilots, because it offered great visibility and a roomy, comfortable cockpit, unlike some of its contemporaries. Yeager found the Thunderbolt to typically be well armed and quite effective in dogfighting. It was definitely one of the airplanes Yeager wanted to experience and get checked out in now that he had a chance to do so. He jumped at the opportunity to fly the heavy bird when it was offered.

On one particular early morning run, he found himself over the Ohio River near Huntington, West Virginia. He suddenly had a wild notion. Hamlin was not that far beyond, and with a quick mental calculation confirming that he had enough fuel to make the round trip, he brought the P-47's nose around, pointing her in the direction of his hometown. He had never seen Hamlin from the air. Now was his chance.

The Thunderbolt, being so heavy, had gained the reputation for being able to dive at speeds approaching the sound barrier. On the other hand, the plane was notoriously slow to climb. Some of the Army Air Forces pilots claimed they had come close to or possibly even reached Mach 1 while diving in combat. There was no way for them to prove it. However, whether climbing or diving, the plane often became difficult to fly.

Once Yeager located Hamlin that morning—the town was more difficult to find and looked even smaller from the air than he had anticipated—he proceeded to have some fun. He dived on the little burg at speeds approaching 500 miles per hour, did barrel rolls shockingly close to the ground, and came close to clipping treetops along the main street as he made several very loud and very-low-altitude passes over the area. All this at about seven o'clock in the morning. Then, his homecoming complete and getting low on fuel, he flew on back to Wright Field, chuckling to himself about the show he had put on for the home folks. Back at the base, he climbed into a waiting P-39 to resume putting its new propeller through its paces. He had no idea of the chaos he had unleashed back home.

That night, when he called his folks, Yeager learned of the mess his little flyover had caused in Hamlin. People were running through the streets in a panic, not sure what kind of aerial attack had broken out. Some thought the Germans were launching an aerial bombardment. One woman suffered a possible heart attack and ended up in the hospital. Farmers claimed the airplane had led to miscarriages among their pregnant stock and that a mule had run off in fright, dragging its plow behind, ruining much of its owner's crop. Another said the thunderous, low-flying aircraft had leveled a complete field of corn.

Yeager's parents were angry with him, too. Once the crazy pilot flew away and things settled down, everybody in town realized who was likely responsible for such destructive mischief. Hal Yeager's boy was at the time the only active fighter pilot from Lincoln County. It had to have been him!

That did not stop Chuck from amusing himself on subsequent visits. He buzzed his town, and especially the homes of family members—including Grandpa Yeager—several more times during his brief duty at Wright Field. He would later maintain that the folks down there came to enjoy the free air show. He flew beneath the Kanawha Bridge—to the consternation of people in boats on the river and in cars on the bridge—and there were unsubstantiated rumors he flew under several other bridges, too. There is no record of anyone complaining to the Army. It was certainly not the first or last time Yeager had some fun in an airplane, to the considerable alarm and dismay of folks on the ground.

When his brief tenure as a test pilot was completed, Flight Officer Yeager headed back west to catch up with his squadron. He arrived by train just as everyone else was getting to Oroville, a small town known as the "City of Gold" for its role in the California gold rush. This two-month stay would be their next-to-last stop before going to war, and Chuck and his contemporaries intended to make the most of it. That included not only their training but also whatever social life this little Sierra Nevada mining town might offer.

On their very first day there, he and a fellow pilot decided they should have a dance and party to welcome the young heroes of the 357th to the area. They boldly headed over to the base's United Service Organizations (USO) office to get the ball rolling.

Yeager was immediately smitten with the beautiful young lady who had the job of social director for the local USO. But it did not go well when the two pilots informed her that she needed to arrange for a dance that very evening to welcome about thirty new arrivals to the air base, Oroville, and Butte

County. Though only eighteen years old and a recent high school graduate, the young lady balked, holding her ground against these two brash flyboys.

"No way!" she told them. "I can't possibly round up thirty girls for a dance on such short notice."

"You don't need to find thirty girls," Yeager shot back. "You only need twenty-nine. You're going to be my date for the dance."

Somehow it all worked out. Despite his arrogant manner and the fact that she could hardly understand Yeager's West Virginia twang, Glennis Faye Dickhouse agreed to go as his date to the hastily arranged dance at the Elk's Club that night. The couple soon found they had much in common and became a regular "item," about the only distraction keeping the young pilot's feet on the ground for the next couple of months.

The fact was Chuck Yeager had fallen hard for Glennis Dickhouse the moment he saw her. Like him, she had grown up in a rural setting, on a small ranch in the Sierra Nevada foothills. And, like Chuck, she had learned at an early age how to shoot and hunt, not necessarily for fun but to put food on the family table. Besides, she also had a practical and tough demeanor that made her all the more attractive to him. The feelings appeared to be mutual. Many young men briefly assigned to the base in Oroville had flirted with Glennis already. But they had been there for a dance or two and then gone on to combat. Chuck Yeager was the first for whom she became a regular "drag," trainee slang for "date."

When the inevitable orders came, sending Yeager and his group to Casper, Wyoming, for their final stop stateside, he and

Glennis did what so many other young men and women were doing all over the country. They agreed to stay in touch, to write each other. They exchanged pictures, too. But there were no promises, no commitments. No pact to not see others while the war kept them apart at such great distances, facing so much uncertainty about the future. No one knew how long this war might last. But they certainly realized the odds that a fighter pilot might never return home.

It was common practice for pilots to name their own planes once they were flying into combat. That name would be painted on the nose or fuselage of the aircraft, along with a caricature of some kind. Chuck promised Glennis he would name his first plane after her: *Glamorous Glen*. It was a promise to her that he knew he would keep.

Before he left Oroville, Yeager yet again found himself in hot water. On one of his last days of training there, while flying back to the base from a practice mission, he decided to go home by a roundabout route. It would take him near the basic pilot training base at Chico, California. Sure enough, the newly minted flyboys—most of whom had only recently soloed—were neatly lined up in their trainers for miles out in the approach pattern to the airstrip, patiently waiting for their turn for landing. Without regard for procedure or protocol, Yeager decided to have some fun with them. He proceeded to give them some grief, zipping in out of the sun so they would not see him coming, flying frighteningly close to them, doing barrel rolls and sharp turns to just miss them, and finally conducting mock dogfights with the terrified novices.

When he finally had had enough fun, he flew on and touched

down on the runway at Oroville. That was when he realized one of the trainer planes had followed and landed right behind him. It turned out to be the commander of the Chico base, a colonel, who had been flying along with his trainees. He was livid. After giving Yeager a tongue-lashing, the colonel went into flight headquarters, threatening to have him court-martialed. If not drawn and quartered.

Luckily, the men of the 357th moved on after another day or two and Yeager left that latest bit of unpleasantness far behind him. At least as far as he knew. He still worried that the colonel might be angry enough and have enough clout that he could get Yeager grounded, keeping him out of the war. At least in a fighter plane. He was sure the Army could bust him back to private and find a rifle and backpack for him. However, he never heard any more about the incident and it became one of his favorite stories to tell.

He would later write that he did not enjoy his stay at Oroville, other than meeting the woman who would one day become his wife and the love of his life. The town obviously felt more positive about what would become one of its most famous temporary residents. Today, Oroville Municipal Airport, which is made up of the former Army Air Forces training base, is located at 225 Chuck Yeager Way, a side street off Oro Dam Boulevard leading to the terminal building and hangars.

Next, the impish young pilot found himself in Casper, Wyoming—moving from the "Gold City" to the "Oil City"—in September of 1943, just as the chill winds were beginning to blow in from the north, up near the Crow and Cheyenne reservations. The base at Casper had been hastily constructed the previous autumn, but by the time Yeager's group arrived, it consisted of more than four hundred buildings, designed to house as many as 20,000 men over the next few years. Still, most of the barracks were heated by coal stoves and their thin walls and leaky seams did little to keep that brisk wind from finding its way inside.

The base's primary purpose was to train bomber crews for combat on both fronts, starting with B-17s and later adding B-24s. That also made it the perfect place to give fighter pilots their final tune-up for running interference for those big aircraft. Most of the trainees were there for a short period of time, looking to learn whatever they needed, then finally move on to where the fight was. Staring at that imposing future, the men wanted to have a good time and blow off some steam while they were off duty, too.

That meant the usual bars and fights and more USO dances. But some of the men, including Chuck Yeager, also enjoyed spending time in the rugged outdoors in the area. Still, a drawing that appeared in the local newspaper depicted some of the airmen dancing with local girls at one of the events. But the trainees were depicted as having the heads of wolves. That was the image most of the citizens of Casper had of the transient airmen.

Chuck Yeager partook in all the off-duty activities, but he still missed Glennis. At one point they arranged to meet up in Reno, Nevada. She got there ahead of him and checked into the hotel. But Chuck failed to show. An angry Glennis finally got in touch by phone with one of his buddies at the air base in Casper. There was a very good reason why he had failed to make the romantic rendezvous.

Earlier in the day, Chuck was taking part in an exercise, staging a practice attack on a group of B-24s. As he was darting in for a "kill," his airplane suddenly and inexplicably exploded, literally coming apart in midair. He managed to bail out, but when the parachute opened, it knocked him unconscious. He did not remember anything after that.

A sheep rancher found him mostly covered by his parachute on the crest of a hill, assumed he was dead, and strapped him across his burro. The rancher later realized Yeager was still alive when he heard him groan. He took him straight to a hospital. Instead of spending the next few days with Glennis at the Kit Carson Hotel in Reno, he was laid up in a hospital bed with a fractured back. The time together in Nevada was not to be.

The injury meant another trip was in jeopardy, too. He could only hope this incident would not delay his heading off to war with his classmates.

The two did manage to get together later. This time it was in Casper, and only a couple of days before he was to ship out. He had convinced the Army that his back was just fine. However, when Glennis first saw him, she could tell it was still bothering him. Even as they danced the night away at a hotel there. And enjoyed antelope steaks with his squadron mates. Every one of the animals that made up the fine meal had been shot by Yeager himself as he "convalesced." Then, after saying a final goodbye, Glennis returned to Oroville while Chuck prepared to take the train cross country to New York City and the ship that would transport him to Europe and the war.

Neither of them could have known that Chuck's mishap and dangerous escape was only a forewarning of what was about to happen once he began flying real missions across the English Channel, into occupied France, and in the skies over Germany. Or just how unpromising his first few months of fighting for his country would be.

FIVE

"DOING WHAT I WAS BORN TO DO"

I'm a fatalist, if that's what you call it. Maybe that helped me in war. If you can't do anything about it, forget it.

—Chuck Yeager, responding to a question on how he felt about so often facing death during his career

RMS *Queen Elizabeth*, sister ocean liner to the legendary *Queen Mary*, was launched in September of 1938 and, buoyed by high expectations, promptly began sea trials. The elegant vessel had been constructed by the Cunard Line to carry passengers back and forth across the Atlantic in luxury, making the run between Southampton, England, and New York City with an interim stop each way in Cherbourg, France. At the time, she was the largest such vessel ever built, if not one of the most opulent. Would-be travelers on both sides of the ocean excitedly awaited her maiden round-trip voyage, scheduled to begin with a festive sailing from Great Britain on April 24, 1940.

That didn't happen. With the onset of World War II, that voyage was indefinitely postponed, and the liner's sea trials and final fitting-out came to an abrupt halt. The massive new ship sat at the dock near where she had been built at Clydebank,

Scotland, near Glasgow, with the bright, happy Cunard colors still determinedly flying from every flagpole.

Then urgent orders came from Britain's First Lord of the Admiralty, a gentleman named Winston Churchill, that the ship was to vacate Clydebank immediately. There was fear, based on intercepted intelligence reports, that German spies and saboteurs might attempt to hit the ship before she could be converted to some other useful purpose, one that could be used against the Third Reich.

As part of her sudden disembarkation, all efforts were undertaken to make the Germans believe that the *Queen Elizabeth* was bound for her originally intended destination, down the Firth of Clyde, along the western coast of Scotland, to the port of Southampton on the southern shores of Great Britain. That included the British navy booking hotel rooms in Southampton in the names of many of the ship's crew members. Instead, once away from the dock at Clydebank, the big ship's crew steered her westward, north of Ireland, bound for New York, in the United States of America, which was, at that time, still a neutral party in the war. She ran an erratic course while maintaining top speed—about twenty-six knots—all the way across the Atlantic to try to avoid German U-boats.

As it turned out, it was a good thing the massive ship had not gone to Southampton as planned. Luftwaffe bombers pounded the port for several nights straight at about the time she would have shown up there had she not made that hard course correction toward the United States.

From New York Harbor, and after a few weeks in port, she steamed much farther west, to Singapore, for shipyard work to convert the fancy passenger vessel to serve instead as a troopship. Her initial job was to ferry Australian soldiers and war equipment around the Pacific. Later, beginning in March of 1942—now painted gray and sporting antiaircraft guns—she began crisscrossing the Atlantic once again, this time carrying American troops to Europe on the eastbound voyage and returning westward, bringing home those who had served their time in battle or been wounded.

The original German intelligence reports turned out to be correct. The British had found a way for the luxurious ocean liner to valiantly serve the war effort against Hitler and his Third Reich.

Along with her sister, the *Queen Mary*, which performed similar duty during the war, the *Queen Elizabeth* often traveled without an escort, since the vessel's top speed enabled it to outrun the German submarines. In all, while serving as a troopship throughout most of World War II, the *Queen Elizabeth* sailed more than a half million miles and provided transportation for greater than 750,000 military personnel.

One of those was Flight Officer Charles Elwood Yeager of Hamlin, West Virginia. We have few recollections from Yeager about his trip, but we can assume he was impressed with the size of the vessel. Almost certainly her huge engines and other modern mechanical systems.

As Chuck had promised when he and Glennis parted a few days before he left Wyoming, he called often and the two kept up a regular correspondence, with Yeager keeping Glennis posted on every detail up to the day the ship finally left New York Harbor. After that, the phone calls ceased and letters would show up less often, usually with whole passages marked out by censors in ugly black blotches. But she did learn that Chuck, as supply officer for the 357th Fighter Squadron, remained behind in Casper for a few days after the rest of his bunch had left in order to arrange for shipping all their gear. That included a load of washing machines that would make the voyage with them. And Yeager had made certain those washers were packed with more than 500 pounds of candy for the kids in England.

Once Chuck caught up with his squadron, they set sail on Tuesday, November 23, 1943. After all that training and getting ready and then still more training, they were finally bound for the war, where they hoped to help make a difference. They were excited about the possibilities. As they proceeded to cross the Atlantic, leaving New York and the Statue of Liberty behind them, they would not have known November 23 was already a busy time for the team they were about to join. During bombing raids that night, the historic German Opera House and the famous Berlin Zoo were destroyed. More than 4,000 animals died in the attack on the zoo.

The Atlantic crossing was uneventful. A few weeks later, Yeager and his group finally arrived at the place where they would spend the balance of their time—about thirteen months—while stationed in Great Britain. It was the Royal Air Force station at Leiston, in Suffolk, located on England's east coast, directly across the lower reaches of the North Sea and upper part of the English Channel from Amsterdam and The Hague in the Netherlands.

Leiston was a relatively new facility. The RAF had only

completed construction and allocated the airfield to the US Army Air Forces two months earlier, in September. And although Yeager's squadron was among the first to move in, Leiston was already a very busy place. The base had seen its first aircraft arrivals even before its runways had been completed. They had not been routine landings, though. The previous July, two heavily damaged B-17 Flying Fortress bombers had put wheels down there, both at different times but on the same day, barely missing some personnel and construction vehicles as well as tree stumps that had not yet been removed from the marshy land.

That would happen repeatedly throughout the war. The base was one of the closest to the action—only three miles inland from the chilly waters of the North Sea—and it would often serve as a first and only viable option for an emergency landing by shot-up aircraft of all types. Never mind that the base was often socked in by thick fog. The crews of those damaged planes did not care about that as long as they were able to find a runway. But the pea soup was often a problem for returning fighters—damaged or not—who would resort to landing blindly, employing prayer, radio guidance, and sheer luck when the visibility occasionally fell to less than fifty feet.

The 357th joined other squadrons as part of the newly formed Eighth Air Force. Confident they finally had the right combination of aircraft, crews, and intelligence to resume around-the-clock bombing deep into the Continent, all the way to Germany, the Army Air Forces were set to take the war right to Hitler's doorstep. They soon learned that the Führer was fully aware of what was going on.

The nearest town to the base was a small village named Yox-ford. Yeager and his squad quickly began calling themselves the "Yoxford Boys." They soon proudly drank to the moniker when they began frequenting the pubs nearby. They were surprised a few days later when they caught a broadcast on the radio from Berlin, welcoming the Yoxford Boys to England and the war and promising them a short but tragic end if they dared to fly into German-occupied airspace.

True to their extensive training, the primary mission of Yeager's squadron—and most of the others based at Leiston—would be to escort Army Air Forces bombers deep into Europe, including the skies over Germany and all the way to Berlin. That would be a round trip of about 1,200 miles, about the same distance as a flight from New York to Miami. The missions for the fighter craft would often be to shield the heavy bombers as they conducted around-the-clock precision bombing runs, including in full daylight. Later, as the Luftwaffe lost more and more planes and pilots, the American fighter planes would be able to leave their escort jobs and seek out targets on the ground. But even as elements of the German air force dwindled, it would remain hazardous duty as Yeager and his brothers encountered and took on an enemy that was growing more and more desperate.

Fortunately, though, the pilots in Yeager's squad would be flying the best and latest fighter-bomber plane available for the job. That was the North American Aircraft P-51B Mustang. And they would be among the first American pilots to fly that particular warbird into combat.

As the British Royal Air Force realized early on when they

scarfed up all the original P-51 Mustangs they could buy before the war even started, this fighter was perfectly suited for air-to-air combat and running interference for mainly B-17 Flying Fortress and B-24 Liberator bombers. The Mustangs made an immediate impact on the success of bombing missions, with results going from dismal to remarkable. Experimentation continued and later versions of the P-51 became even more capable and versatile.

Before that, the British had stopped all daytime bombing runs after suffering heavy losses. The Americans persisted, convinced that tightly packed formations of bombers could defend themselves. They soon learned differently. Those runs amounted to little more than suicide missions. At that time, Allied bombers were being escorted by P-38 Lightning and P-47 Thunderbolt aircraft. Both planes were perfectly capable fighters but with one serious limitation: their range and altitude capabilities. Even under typical conditions, they only had about four hours of flight time before they ran out of fuel. And, as previously noted, they were not very good at greater than about 15,000 feet. The newer P-51 Mustangs, however, came equipped with wing tanks and could fly twice as long. And a new development allowed them to operate well at more than 30,000 feet in altitude.

By the time Chuck Yeager made his first combat mission from Leiston on February 11, 1944, the Mustangs had mostly been switched to the Rolls-Royce "Merlin" engines. They had a special turbocharger that dramatically improved capability of the plane while operating above about 15,000 feet, the altitude at which the original motors on the P-38s, P-47s, and original Mustangs became grossly underpowered. They also gave the P-51 a top level-flight speed of over 400 miles per hour. And armed with six .50-caliber M2 Browning machine guns, the improved Mustang would quickly become the best tool available for the task.

Best but not perfect. The pilots who flew them—including Chuck Yeager—noted that they could be tricky to control. With all that speed and maneuverability, the aircraft was a dogfighter's dream. It offered almost too much flexibility for some pilots to handle. Much of this was attributed to its specialized wing design. Also, if an enemy shot happened to hit the plane's coolant system, which was wonderfully efficient but quite vulnerable, there was no saving the aircraft. It quickly lost the engine and became a powerless glider. The pilot had no option but to bail out and hope for the best. This issue was especially crucial when the Mustang was used more and more to strafe ground targets, often down to treetop level. Even small-arms fire could damage that cooling system and take down the plane and its pilot.

But even with those limitations, the German Luftwaffe had few answers for the P-51B. They originally employed their heavy fighter plane, the Messerschmitt Bf 110, which so far had enjoyed great success against the Allied bombers and previous escorting fighter planes. But they were no match for the Mustang and were soon grounded, often involuntarily. Their Focke-Wulf Fw 190 aircraft and the Messerschmitt Me 109 were generally considered to be equal to the Mustang in most respects, even superior in a couple more.

But those aircraft lacked one of the same important capabilities as the American P-38s and P-47s. That was range. Once the separate ejectable fuel tanks were added to the American P-51 fighter planes, it gave their pilots the ability to outlast the enemy in dogfights even while escorting bombers deep into Germany. The Germans would have to abandon the battle when their fighter planes became thirsty, racing off to try to find a landing strip somewhere, often with the Army Air Forces Mustangs in hot pursuit.

One of Germany's highest-scoring fighter pilots, Heinz Bär, would later be quoted as saying, "The P-51 was perhaps the most difficult of all Allied aircraft to meet in combat. It was fast, maneuverable, hard to see, and difficult to identify because it closely resembled the Me 109."

There was one other development that would affect how Yeager and his squadron fought their airplanes. About the time they were making the Atlantic crossing on the *Queen Elizabeth*, Major General James H. Doolittle, the new commander of the Eighth Air Force, ordered a different tactic be adopted by his fighter pilots. Doolittle was already famous for leading a group of B-25 bombers off the decks of the carrier USS *Hornet* (CV-8) in April of 1942 to drop bombs on the Japanese Home Islands, including Tokyo. He did so while knowing the planes might well not have a safe place to land afterward, that it would likely be a one-way mission. However, the value of such an audacious attack on the empire so early in the war made it worth the risk. The biggest morale win was that the Japanese now knew that if the Americans could bomb the Home Islands, they could drop a bomb on their emperor, who was viewed as a sacred entity.

Indeed, Jimmy Doolittle had to bail out of his own B-25 and drifted down into a rice paddy in China. Fortunately he was rescued by the Chinese and made it back home. Those historic raids did little physical damage to targets in Japan but had a major psychological effect, negatively on the Japanese and positively on the morale of the United States, which had had little good news from the war effort to that point. By the time Doolittle moved halfway around the world to command the Eighth Air Force in Europe, he had already been presented the Medal of Honor by President Franklin Roosevelt for that historic and daring mission.

Now, in his new command, Major General Doolittle decided it was time to divert other resources to achieve air supremacy over the Luftwaffe. Part of accomplishing that goal was to take some of his fighter planes away from close-by escort duty and have them run out miles ahead of the bomber formations. They were to greet the German aircraft wherever they found them as they left the ground and scrambled to get in formations to take on the approaching Allied bombers. The American pilots no longer had to wait for the Germans to launch their attacks. They began to engage them in air-to-air combat much earlier in the mission, often before the enemy planes had even lined up in formation. Or, if they encountered no enemy planes in the sky, the P-51s were to look for them on the ground. In other words, they were to find and destroy the enemy wherever they encountered them.

There was another important reason for attempting to establish such air superiority, especially in occupied France. As 1944 began, preparations were well underway for the massive

Allied invasion at Normandy—Operation Overlord, or D-Day—already scheduled for early June. Controlling the skies over the beaches there for the initial landing, and then for the subsequent movement of the invasion forces deeper into France, would be an important factor in the outcome of the assault.

By the time Yeager's group was settled in at Leiston and had their Mustangs in the air, the Allies had already increased the number of their bombing missions dramatically and were having more success than previously. That included expanding daytime raids all the way to Berlin, beginning in March of 1944. The P-51B fighters and the twenty-year-olds who were flying them were doing just what the men had promised each other that they would do during all that drilling and practicing back in the skies of California, Arizona, and Nevada. They were making a difference in the war.

And it was a major difference. In the fall of 1943, before the P-51Bs were regularly flying escort, almost 10 percent of all bombers that went out on missions failed to return home. Even more telling, nearly 50 percent came back damaged, more or less seriously. By the time Yeager flew his first mission in his Mustang, in February of 1944, the loss of bombers had dropped to less than 3 percent and only about a third of the big planes were returning from their missions with damage. And that was despite a dramatic increase not only in the number of American bombing runs but also in the number of missions during daylight hours. By spring 1944, Germany was being bombed almost every day and at all hours.

The Germans were countering all this as best they could. Their Focke-Wulf Fw 190 and Messerschmitt Me 109 fighters were, as mentioned, almost the equal of the Mustangs in actual dogfighting ability as well as the capacity to strike and do damage to bomber formations. They remained deadly adversaries against the Allies. The Luftwaffe was also busily developing new and better warplanes, aiming for more speed and flexibility.

That included the futuristic Messerschmitt Me 163B Komet, the only rocket-powered fighter plane ever put into operation. It was designed to intercept enemy aircraft, hit quickly, and then blaze away, with a top speed of greater than 600 miles per hour, its designers claimed. However, the Komet proved to be a tragic bust. Many Luftwaffe test pilots died during its development. The fuel used for its rocket engine was very volatile and corrosive, deadly to pilots and ground crews, and since it was designed to land unpowered with its motor extinguished, pilots had only one chance to get the plane down safely. While a total of about three hundred Komets were built, far fewer ever actually saw service in combat. They tallied only eighteen Allied planes destroyed, with ten Komets shot down.

Another example of new technology developed by the Luftwaffe presented a far greater threat. That was the jet-powered Messerschmitt Me 262 Schwalbe ("Swallow"). Air forces around the world were rushing to develop engines like the Junkers Jumo 004 jet engines on the Me 262, but the Germans were among the first to get a practical design, and the Me 262 became the world's first jet fighter, introduced in the summer of 1944. Its speed was its greatest advantage: it was capable of flying well above 500 miles per hour in level flight—so fast that bomb racks and other attachments were sometimes ripped right off the plane's fuselage. Early on, Hitler was convinced the jet would be a primary defensive weapon when the expected Allied invasion came.

The plane did cause great concern for US pilots. And for good reason: Me 262 pilots claimed to have shot down more than 500 Allied planes. But the jet's limitations were soon discovered and exploited. Strategic bombing took out storage tanks where the specialized jet fuel was kept, as well as factories where the planes were constructed. The Swallow was also very vulnerable while landing or taking off due to the loss of thrust in its engines at relatively slow speeds.

Chuck Yeager would be among the first to take advantage of that vulnerability later in 1944.

At about the same time as Doolittle's alterations in the thrust of the air war, and once Yeager had a chance to meld body and machine in the cockpit of his own Mustang—immediately christened and properly painted up with the name *Glamorous Glen*—Yeager was, in his own words, "doing what I was born to do." He was confident he would do it well.

He had quickly settled into the routine and was ready when his first mission day rolled around. It began at 0530 with a coldwater shave. There was rarely hot water available. But the shave was essential to avoid irritation from the oxygen mask he would be wearing for the next six or seven hours.

Most of the pilots rode bicycles in the cold predawn darkness from their base quarters over to a building where the mission briefing was held. Yeager would soon learn that those briefings varied little from day to day. The details that were most important—takeoff time, where they would meet up with the bombers they were to escort, what the bombers' targets were to be, the route they were to take on the return trip, how much time they had, and the territory they could cover for freelancing and looking for enemy planes on their own—were typically the only mission-to-mission changes. The rest of the briefing would typically be the same every morning. That included the weather forecast. It was always bad this time of year.

Next, Yeager and his fellow pilots pedaled their bikes over to the operations building, where they put on their flight suits, including strapping on a pistol and claiming a parachute. Then, with their helmets and goggles already on their heads, they hastily gobbled up what passed for a preflight breakfast. That was typically hard bread with butter and jam and a quick couple of cups of black coffee.

The final thing to be certain to do before riding a vehicle of some kind out to the flight line was to urinate. Yeager would later write of the importance of that step. Although the cockpit of his fighter was equipped with an elimination tube, it usually froze up at the altitudes they would be flying, frequently at 30,000 feet or higher. A pilot did not need the distraction of a full bladder—or worse—in the middle of a confrontation with a swarm of Luftwaffe commander in chief Hermann Göring's finest fighter pilots.

Yeager would remember being uncharacteristically "scared to death" as he sat there on the flight line that overcast morning in February of 1944, his stomach full of butterflies. Now, after all that preparation, he was about to make his first run, face enemy fire for the first time, maybe engage somebody besides other trainees, but this time in a for-real dogfight. But once

Glamorous Glen's engine was rumbling and he began the roll out to the runway, two by two with his squad, that apprehension quickly faded. The typical Yeager bravado was back. He was looking forward to facing those heralded and aggressive German pilots and their supposedly fine fighters. He knew he was up to the task and convinced that both he and his airplane were superior to anything Hitler could put up there against him. Ground fire did not worry him. He would be hard to hit way up where he would be flying. As he steered his plane onto the runway that gray morning, he was supremely confident he could outfly any man jack he might spar with up there.

Besides, that first mission promised to be a relatively easy one. Once they were wheels-up shortly after 0800, they were to head out over the North Sea, take a right-hand turn down over the English Channel, and then conduct a sweep of the French coast. Although we do not know for sure, that run was likely to gather intelligence for the D-Day invasion or to begin to establish the air superiority Major General Doolittle was seeking.

The squad was careful that each airplane climbed, turned, and cruised at the same rate, flying in a predetermined formation and order as if tied together. They formed up into four groups of four planes each, using hand signals to communicate with each other and always maintaining radio silence. That would go by the wayside should the squad go into battle. The enemy would be well enough aware of their presence and the pilots would certainly use their radios to warn and inform their buddies in the frenzy of aerial combat.

On a typical mission, they would have quickly climbed to 28,000 feet as they flew off to rendezvous with the B-17s or

B-24s they would be escorting that day. Despite the heater in the Mustang's cockpit and the brilliant sunshine once they climbed above the clouds, the temperature outside the plane's canopy would be at least 50 degrees below zero. The pilot would feel the cold, especially in his legs and lower body, which would be in shadow. The seat would be far less comfortable than the one in Yeager's old P-39 Airacobra. And he knew that just behind his back, built into the fighter's fuselage, was a tank filled with 85 gallons of highly flammable airplane fuel. It would be there until he had used up all the gas in the two drop tanks, located beneath each wing; then they could be cut loose to fall to the ground far below. Though protected by armor, there was still the chance that the fuselage tank would be hit by gunfire, either from another plane in a dogfight or from the ground. And the weight of the fuel placed in that part of the craft—at least in the first hour or so of its use, while it was still relatively full of gas—would be a factor in the plane's maneuverability and stability. But none of the pilots complained about the danger or the increased load. That extra fuel gave them a decided advantage, the ability to outlast the enemy in a dogfight and the range to make it back across the English Channel and home so they could fly again the next day.

Yeager had hoped to encounter enemy fighters that very first mission, but there were none. He did later admit to a stab of apprehension when he realized that the brown winter landscape down below them was occupied France. And when they flew lower to look for enemy installations and troop movement, they encountered flak from ant-aircraft installations that was close enough to rock their Mustangs. But by the time they

71

landed safely back at the base, every single pilot was bemoaning the lack of action, of having a "dry run." Not a bullet fired from the .50-caliber Brownings. Not a single Nazi Fw 190 or Me 109 sent augering into the black soil of the French countryside.

As Yeager would later write, "Conducting a mission without a dogfight was like taking R&R in London only to find out all the women had been evacuated."

He would get his chance soon enough to prove himself equal to the task. However, his initial success—using 461 rounds of .50-caliber ammo in the process—would still be most of a frustrating month in coming. And then, only one day after the satisfaction and elation of that long-awaited accomplishment, he would be faced with the likelihood that his career as a fighter pilot would be abruptly halted before he could even tally his second confirmed kill, let alone collect enough kills to be designated an "ace" fighter pilot.

Even worse, in the process, the self-described fatalist Chuck Yeager would soon engage in a dogfight with the Grim Reaper himself.

SIX

PRIDE BEFORE THE FALL

I closed up fast and opened fire at 200 yards. I observed
strikes on fuselage and wing roots with pieces flying off . . .
the E/A engin [sic] was smoking and wind-milling.

    —From Yeager's "Encounter Report" of action on
      March 4, 1944

The young fighter pilot from the hills of Appalachia had turned twenty years old on February 13, 1943. He had celebrated by beginning intense training at Luke Field in Arizona, doing the work it took to become a fighter pilot, the things that would help keep him alive and effective once he was "over there."

His next and more profound birthday—his twenty-first—found him two days into his active-duty service, piloting a fighter aircraft over enemy territory in Europe. That was when he made his first mission on behalf of the Army Air Forces. But after that initial run for his squadron on February 11, the next few weeks offered very little for him to be excited about. No "E/As" (enemy aircraft) to skirmish with. But the guys did throw him one hell of a party, one more than fitting for a twenty-first birthday.

Although the jobs they were being asked to do so far were not likely to have him sparring with any Nazi fighter pilots anytime soon, Chuck Yeager remained full of self-confidence. He saw that trait as an asset that would stand him in good stead once the action got considerably more serious. He also was convinced he was better trained and had superior equipment to the pilots he would ultimately face from Hitler's and Göring's Luftwaffe. He had spent about a year practicing dogfighting, air-to-ground gunnery, dive-bombing, skip bombing (skipping a bomb across water to sink a ship much as he had skipped stones across the Mud River as a boy), and more.

Since he had been the maintenance officer for his squadron for much of the training period, he had had the opportunity to test-fly just about every plane that came out of maintenance. He had not had a chance to check out a P-51 before he arrived in Great Britain, though. But once he climbed into the cockpit of one, strapped himself in, and cranked it up, he considered the airplane to be a natural part of him, like an extra set of arms and legs. Plus wings and a powerful engine. He got that first opportunity soon after getting settled in Leiston, delivering the washing machines, and distributing the candy to the kids who lived in the area. That first flight in a Mustang came only a day before his first mission in one of the birds. He and other pilots took a bus ride to a British assembly base and he flew one of them back to Leiston, where he personally inspected the engine and other mechanical components. He was duly impressed. And, of course, he had given the plane a good workout on the short flight over.

"You have to learn real quick," he once said. "And that's the way our pilots were."

Yeager would later modestly proclaim, "I was no better than the rest of the fighter pilots. I had very good eyes, as a lot of guys did, and also could dogfight. But that was just a matter of training and experience."

But he was not nearly so humble around his wing mates, especially when they blew off steam from the day's mission each night in the local pubs when they had the next day off, or in the on-base officers' club when they did not. He often bragged about the damage he was about to inflict on those Messerschmitt jockeys. So did the others in his group. And that made it especially galling when days and then weeks passed with most of the action consisting of zigzagging through flak and occasionally strafing some unlucky vehicle on a lonely and deserted coastal country road below.

In truth, by design, the newcomers were primarily sent each day on patrols like their initial one back on February 11 to ease them into their new type of planes and their life-or-death jobs, which would be coming soon enough. In the meantime they were sweeping the coast of occupied France along the English Channel, then hurrying on back to Leiston each day with few stories to tell and no kills to celebrate. They would do so for the rest of February and into March. And there would be a grand total of only six official missions of any kind during that time.

Finally, though, on March 4, 1944, Yeager and his squadron were deemed ready and able to be inserted into the big game. Their mission—his eighth—on that chilly, gray morning was to rendezvous with and be an escort for a swarm of B-17 bombers bound for central Germany for a daylight mission. It would be a historic one. They were to participate in the first daylight bombing run on Berlin itself. The pilots were primed and ready.

At first the trip was uneventful, although the weather had turned ugly once they were over occupied France. Cumulus clouds towered high above their flight altitude, and the overcast all around them made for some choppy going. Yeager was leading the second group of four fighters, designated as "White Flight." There was a silver lining in all those storm clouds, though. Because of the weather, the Luftwaffe fighters had apparently decided to remain on the ground, assuming that the Allies would be crazy to try to fly that day. That at first appeared to be a good decision by the Germans. Because of the weather, the US bombers bound for Berlin were recalled, their mission aborted.

But one formation—or "box"—consisting of thirty-six B-17s failed to get the message. They continued on through the clouds toward Berlin. That happened to be the group that Chuck Yeager was shielding.

By the time those bombers had dropped their loads on Berlin and turned toward home, Yeager realized he could no longer see two of the other members of White Flight. Only one other plane was visible. The others were likely out there in the weather somewhere, looking for something to shoot at. No matter. There still were no enemy fighters visible, and it looked as if they would have a bumpy but otherwise routine trip back across France and then the English Channel.

However, as their homebound route took them westward

between the cities of Düsseldorf and Cologne, things changed. They were approaching Kassel, the largest city in the German state of Hesse and the location of a major tank production factory. It was a spot they would mark on their charts for future attention. Then Chuck Yeager was the first to spot—despite the thick deck of clouds all around them—a lone enemy fighter, about ten miles out but quickly approaching. None of the bombers or the other P-51 pilot in the formation could see the German plane yet. However, the other Mustang pilot had flown with Yeager enough to know not to doubt him when he made his brief radio report in that distinctive Appalachian drawl of his.

They could soon have much more company, of course. And right now, the lone German was outnumbered. It would be two to one if both escorts dived on him.

The B-17s were flying home in formation at 26,000 feet, fully aware they had accomplished something notable that day. Yeager told the other P-51 pilot to remain with the bombers as they punched in and out of that potholed cloud cover: if there was one enemy plane out there, there could be more Luftwaffe lurking in the overcast. The rest of Yeager's squadron were lost in the gloom. Most likely they had gone on ahead, looking for a dogfight or ground targets to strafe.

Yeager felt a rush of adrenaline as he watched the lone enemy fighter stalking the formation, clearly unaware he had been seen. The new pilot braced himself, eager for his first real action. It came quicker than he realized. Still thinking he had not been spotted, the sneaky Messerschmitt Me 109 pulled up to his right, not far behind the group of bombers and about 2,000 feet below them. That was a preferred tactic by the enemy pilots. Their intent was to take out "tail-end Charlie," the last bird in the American formation. Often, the other escorts were not even aware they were under attack until the first man hit was yelling on the radio. But this kind of attack usually came when there was a full squadron of enemy fighters. When the Allied escort planes broke formation to challenge their attackers, that left the bombers susceptible to the German ordnance.

In this case, it appeared the lone Me 109 had unexpectedly spotted the box of US bombers as they emerged from the clouds. And he might not have yet seen Yeager and his lone wingman in the murk. A flock of bombers with no escorts! The bastard probably thought it was his lucky day.

We will never know if Yeager grinned or whooped or showed any outward sign of elation at the realization that he was about to engage in his first real life-or-death dogfight. But we do know he did not hesitate. All that training and practice told him exactly how he should respond to the sudden appearance of an enemy fighter plane. It bordered on instinct. And from the moment he spied the German, Yeager already was confident he knew how this was going to end.

He abruptly brought the stick of his Mustang hard right and used both feet on the rudder pedals to make *Glamorous Glen* turn suddenly and sharply. Then he put her into a steep dive directly at the Me 109. The German pilot was most likely surprised that he had been spotted before even launching his attack—that he was no longer an unseen stalker. That he was now a target of the P-51 he had not seen before it was already plunging toward him.

The Messerschmitt pilot decided not to fight. He immediately put his airplane into a 50-degree dive. It was clear to Yeager the German wanted no part of a dogfight with a Mustang. The steep dive would give him maximum escape speed to attempt to shake the American suddenly careening in his direction. Surely the Mustang would not chase a single fighter with what already amounted to a good head start. He likely only wanted to scare away the Me 109, then return to formation to resume escorting the bombers. Then the Luftwaffe pilot could either fly on back to base and report his encounter or hide in the clouds, keeping up with the enemy bomber formation, maybe alert other fighters, and eventually sneak back up on their tails and fire on them, his original quarry.

But the German did not know who was at the stick of that P-51. While the rest of the planes, including the other Mustang, flew on, Chuck Yeager went after the Me 109 with teeth bared. He had no intention of simply chasing the German plane away. He was determined to shoot him down.

Yeager goosed the throttle and squared up quickly on the speedily diving Messerschmitt. So the brave Luftwaffe warrior wanted to run away! To go off and hide in the cloud deck!

Yeager did not hesitate nor even consider letting him get away. When he was within about two hundred yards of the target, when he was sure he had the right angle, range, speed, and aim, his instincts screamed, *Now! Now! Now!* He fired a long burst from one of his M2 Browning machine guns and immediately could tell that he had hit home. The bullets pounded into the Me 109's fuselage, right at the point where its wings were attached. Considerable debris flew away, some of it rattling like hailstones against the canopy of Yeager's shiny new Mustang. He was suddenly in the middle of a swarm of scrap metal coming off a disintegrating airplane.

Then he realized that, in his excitement and haste to chase and shoot down the German, he had overestimated his target's speed. He was about to overrun the other plane. If he did not correct course, it would not only put him out of position to get off another volley but would also put him into the sights of the German if he was spoiling for a shootout. Yeager pulled the nose up hard and did a sharp aileron roll to come back around, trying to line up again behind the speeding, diving enemy pilot without stalling his own airplane. The P-51 responded amazingly well.

He could tell he had done damage to the Messerschmitt, but the enemy aircraft still flew straight and with no telltale smoke. He was also still diving at about the same steep but controlled angle, nowhere close to an out-of-control, spinning crash. Yeager would persist. His dad had taught him well that the job was never over until it was completed.

But he also knew he needed to make quick work of it. There could be other attackers appearing out of the thick clouds, approaching the bombers—they were, after all, still over Germany and had just bombed the hell out of Berlin in broad daylight—and there was only one P-51 still up there to try to deflect them. The pilot of the Me 109 might have already informed his buddies of the presence of this nice box of B-17 targets. Still, Yeager was confident he could finish this guy off in only a few more seconds, claim his first kill, and rejoin the formation.

This time he pulled in even closer before he once again

opened fire. Almost at once, the Me 109's engine erupted and began belching ugly black smoke. Then its damaged motor stopped altogether. Even though its propeller was still spinning, or "windmilling," that was only because of the wind as the aircraft hurtled earthward. It was no longer turning at the behest of the now dead and smoking V12 power plant.

With the adrenaline still flowing, Yeager inadvertently flew right past his target yet again. And once more he had to put his plane through a fancy maneuver—this Mustang was one sweet ride!—so he could come around and get in position for another salvo from the .50-caliber. But before he was set up to blast away again, he took a good look at the bullet holes all along the fuselage, the canopy, and the engine cowling of the enemy fighter. And at all the smoke pouring out of its engine compartment.

He did a quick calculation and decided not to waste more ammunition or time on this one. It was a dead duck.

Then, as confirmation that Yeager had his first kill, the canopy suddenly flew off the Me 109 and one of Hitler's fine fighter pilots was literally flung out of his cockpit, tumbling into thin air as his plane fell away. The man's chute was not yet open when he disappeared into thick clouds at about 9,000 feet. No way for Yeager to tell if it ever opened.

Then the hunk of heavy metal that had so recently been a sleek Luftwaffe warplane, still trailing dense smoke, was swallowed up by that same heavy overcast.

Chuck Yeager had just bagged his first E/A! He finally had a "kill"!

But as he circled back around to pick up the formation of

bombers and his escorting buddy—who had also watched and would confirm the shoot-down—he had one disappointment. One he would casually mention on his official report of the incident.

"The E/A took no evasive action after the first burst," he would write. He had hoped for so much more in his first air-to-air encounter with the enemy.

There had been no opportunity to shoot it out with the bastard! No chance to outfly and outshoot one of the Luftwaffe's supposedly superior fighter pilots. The enemy flyer could have been wounded, just able to pull the canopy release and get out. Or he could have known his ride was damaged after the first salvo, that it could not be effective in a dogfight, and he was trying to escape and save himself and his plane. Regardless, in his report, Yeager would not make any claim that he took out the pilot. Only "one Me 109."

That day's mission was not over, though. On the trip home, he spotted a German light bomber far below him and immediately dived on the target. Although the plane had a top-turret and rear gunner, they apparently did not spot the Mustang rocketing out of the storm clouds. Yeager got off a volley that he was certain did damage and likely took out the tail gunner. But just then the plane disappeared into those same problematic black clouds.

No way to pursue. No means to confirm either damage or a kill.

Finding home was usually a problem, too. They carried no navigational gear on the Mustangs beyond a simple compass. Yeager would later say, "We knew England was west of Germany, so we flew west until we saw the English Channel. Then we flew low until we found a base. Any base. There was a bomber base, an RAF base, some kind of air base every ten miles [along the coast]. And since we were usually low on fuel by then, we landed at the first base we came to, got fuel, and then flew on to Leiston."

His disappointment in his first kill not coming as part of a spectacular dogfight would soon get washed away with plenty of drink. That and the opportunity once they were back to Leiston to recount the action in detail and celebrate his big day. Yes, there would be a party at the little Nissen hut that had been designated as the officers' club, a place where each day's exploits were rehashed over Spam sandwiches and gallons of Scotch. They could also drink to the success of the first daylight bombing raid by the Allies of Berlin. Yeager and his flight of fighters had done their part that day to get Hitler's attention!

His most often quoted remark when, in later life, he was asked about that initial wartime kill?

"It was a lot easier than I thought it would be."

After he had time to sober up and reflect, Yeager would also admit being surprised that he did not feel bad at all that he had so violently ended the day—and maybe the war, and even possibly the life—of a fellow fighter pilot. And likely the life of the tail gunner in that bomber, too. This was war. He was doing what he had been trained to do up there, 26,000 feet above the lovely city of Kassel. So was the German aviator and the kid in that rear bubble. Trying to keep the Americans from dropping bombs on crucial war matériel factories down below. (During bombing on Kassel in World War II, more than 10,000 people died, 90 percent of the historic and beautiful downtown area was destroyed, and more than 150,000 people were left homeless. But there was never more than minimal damage done to the tank factory, the primary target of the bombing raids.)

He would later tell a reporter, "An enemy is just a guy who you have to kill."

Despite his initial disappointment, Yeager would also become more philosophical about his first chance at real aerial combat. On that day he had been quicker, luckier, and more sharp-eyed than his counterpart. And it was Yeager who won the skirmish. Another day? Another fight? It could have been a very different outcome.

And Chuck Yeager—proudly looking forward to flying his eighth mission the very next morning—would soon learn how real that possibility was.

SEVEN

"TAIL-END CHARLIE"

I got out at 18,000 feet. I was whirling on [my] back so I pulled cord at 8,000 feet. An Fw 190 above me started toward me. As he was about 2,000 yards from me, a 51 came in on his tail and blew him up.

—Chuck Yeager, in his handwritten official report on being shot down over occupied France

Chuck Yeager might have been nursing a bit of a hangover as he and the squad gathered for their mission briefing in the early-morning chill of March 5, 1944. But despite all the boisterous celebrating the night before of his first enemy plane shot down, he was up, fresh, bright, and ready to go do it again.

Nothing different from the previous day. Getting ready. Final briefing. Takeoff at 0800. Eighteen Mustangs. Rendezvous with their wing mates. Fly in formation to their designated coordinates. Meet up there with the B-24 bombers that would be bound on this run for Bordeaux, France. Escort them safely for a daylight bombing raid on several targets, including hitting that occupied city, and attempt to do damage to vital targets that so far had proven to be maddeningly challenging.

Bordeaux is famous for its wine production and more than 350 architectural monuments, and the area was not what many would consider a worthy bombing target for the Allies. But the town is located on the Garonne River, which offers a deep shipping channel from its port facilities out to the Atlantic Ocean. At one point in the city's history, it was the world's second busiest seaport, surpassed only by London. For that reason, in World War II, its harbor became the home port of the German 12th U-boat Flotilla. That made the submarine pens a frequent but, as it turned out, frustrating target. Because of their massive and heavily reinforced concrete construction, they were practically impervious to the Allies' best shots. And they certainly tried. Tried and failed. No significant damage was ever done to the facilities or the dreaded U-boats in port there.

This day would prove no different. But this mission would soon throw Chuck Yeager a major curveball. One that would threaten to end not only his career as a fighter pilot but his life.

All was going according to the briefing plan. By 12:40 in the afternoon, they were about fifty miles north of their targets, already over the department of Gironde, of which Bordeaux was the capital. No one had challenged them so far, even though they had veered just off course to bomb a German airdrome at the town of Angoulême. But that successful effort was the equivalent of kicking a hornet's nest.

Yeager was flying in the most unenviable position in the formation, bringing up the rear, a spot termed "tail-end Charlie." That had not been the original plan. As usual, luck played a role. On this day Yeager was flying as a "spare." Once they met up with the formation of bombers and flew on toward the mission, if none of the other escort planes had encountered any problems, the "spare" would return to base. On this morning the extra aircraft would be needed. One of the other P-51s had engine problems. He was sent back to base. Yeager dutifully swung around to bring up the rear in his place as part of "Green Flight."

Then, as had happened the day before, the enemy employed their favorite maneuver. This time, though, it was a horde of Germans that sneaked up from behind and above the formation without being seen. With the element of surprise on their side, they swooped in to pick off the Allied fighters one at a time, starting with the unfortunate soul who was flying as tail-end Charlie, opening up the bombers for attack.

The tactic worked perfectly on that March morning above the vineyards of Bordeaux. Yeager was taken completely by surprise. It was too late to do much to get out of their way. He just had enough time to key the radio.

"Cement Green leader," he said, using the designated name for the group on this mission. "Three bogies at five o'clock. Break right. Break right."

But the Germans were already shooting at Yeager and his Mustang. He was in mid–avoidance maneuver when the first shots of 20mm rounds slammed into *Glamorous Glen*.

"3 Fw 190s came in from the rear," he later wrote in his official recap of the incident. "Seared [*sic*: severed] elevator cables."

That gave Yeager little control over his Mustang. But the Focke-Wulf pilots were not through, nor was that the extent of the damage. They sent another stream of 20mm ordnance into the P-51's engine. The plane skewed sideways and there was immediately a plume of smoke and a surge of fire.

There was no saving the airplane now. Although he had no power whatsoever from what was left of his nearly 1,800-horsepower engine, Yeager managed to jump on the rudder control peddles and do a snap roll, leaving him upside down. That made it easier for him to get out of the aircraft. He glanced at the altimeter: 18,000 feet. At the rate the plane was falling, he would be at least 2,000 feet closer to planet Earth by the time he could finally get unbuckled, get out of the cockpit, and be free-falling.

As it turned out, he did not have to jettison the plane's canopy. It had been hit and simply fell away once he was inverted. And Yeager tumbled out of the cockpit, aided by the pull of gravity but bumping his head hard on something in the process. Before he knew it, he was tumbling downward, almost three miles above the special dirt that was so prized for the wine grapes it nurtured.

As he fell, spinning wildly, and even though he was dizzy and disoriented, he managed to disconnect and discard all the gear that remained strapped to his body. That included the heavy pack that held a small, inflatable dinghy, just in case he landed in the sea; his oxygen mask, which he no longer needed; and his leather flight helmet. He tossed it all away. Instinct told him to grab the ring that was attached to the ripcord and open the parachute lashed to his back. And do it as soon as he could. But he fought the impulse. And for good reason.

When he managed to stop tumbling, he looked up to where

he had been flying his P-51 alongside his wing mates and the bombers only moments before. The big Flying Fortresses were now distant dots of black against the white clouds. The German fighters and his brothers from the 363rd Fighter Squadron were buzzing about, brawling with each other. He could hear the distant humming, rattling, and booming of the skirmish as he jerked around to see it. Although he was still falling, he wanted to try to determine if one of the Fw 190s that had so sneakily taken him out—before he could even engage in a little honest-to-goodness dogfighting—might be following his plunge with the intent of zooming in and finishing him off.

Rumor had it that once a pilot had had his airplane shot out from under him, the Luftwaffe pilots would sometimes do just that: follow the poor guy down, wait until he opened his chute and slowed his descent, and then use their 20mm guns to make sure that airman never escorted another bomber. This rumor was later found to be false. There were no reports of any pilots parachuting out of their damaged airplanes and then being shot by the German pilots.

Of course, Yeager did not know that as he free-fell toward Bordeaux. But he would make it a point to tell many interviewers in the ensuing years that there was at least a bit of professional courtesy up there in those dangerous skies.

There was, however, a well-founded reason to fear bullets coming at him from another direction. And another reason to not pull the rip cord until he absolutely had to. Any Germans—or French who were loyal to the Führer—would have heard the action high above them. They absolutely would wait patiently until any shot-down Allied pilots opened their parachutes and thus became easy, dangling bull's-eyes. Then they would take target practice on them. And some of the French farmers, to curry favor with their occupiers, would use either their pitchforks or scythes to stab or hack the flyers to death, or capture them and turn them over for bounties.

So Yeager knew to be prudent, no matter how desperately he wanted to jerk that rip cord. Instead, he hoped to postpone deploying his lifesaving chute until the very last moment. That would make him a small target and keep him descending rapidly when he was most vulnerable.

The tumbling and spinning were the hard part. He was growing dizzy, disoriented. He knew there was real danger that he might black out. If so, he would never wake up. He could also now see details of features on the ground as they rushed up to meet him.

"I was whirling on [my] back so I pulled [the] cord at 8000 feet," he later reported. The parachute spilled from its pack and quickly inflated above him, slowing his fall, but it was also advertising his presence in the sky while he was still a mile and a half above the vineyards and farmland.

Almost immediately after the parachute opened, he heard the whining of a Focke-Wulf Fw 190. He spun around and, sure enough, there he was. He was racing toward the little patch of sky where Yeager swayed beneath his parachute like bait on a hook at the end of a fishing line.

But before the German had a chance to open fire—if he ever had any intention of doing so—Yeager heard another and much more familiar sound. The throaty roar of a Mustang in full-power dive. The Luftwaffe pilot obviously never saw the P-51 zooming in from behind him. Not until the Fw 190 was afire and coming apart in the bright midday sky. The canopy on the German plane never opened. Not the entire time Yeager watched the smoking aircraft spin, tumble, and ultimately slam into a grapevine-covered hillside far below.

The Mustang had already turned, waggled a "Good luck" with its wings, and climbed back to altitude to rejoin the action way up there.

Now Yeager could see the smoke from the crash of his own airplane down there in a stand of trees. Those woods, he knew, could easily be crawling with German soldiers. And their French sympathizers, who did not wear uniforms with swastikas on the sleeves. They were not so easily identified but were just as lethal toward downed American pilots.

He could also smell the earth now. The aroma of the lush forests. For a moment he was homesick for the woods in West Virginia. It also occurred to him that if he somehow survived this jump, if he managed to evade the enemy, he would have to rely on many of the skills he had acquired as a boy in those mountains back home. The ones learned from his dad as well as Grandpa Yeager. Survival skills. Because now that he was growing closer to those woods, surviving was the only thing on his mind.

As he neared the end of his descent, he had no idea just how soon one of those survival skills would be put to good use. As he had been taught in all those basic training classrooms, he manipulated the shroud lines of the chute to try to steer toward

CHUCK YEAGER

a clearing. Many pilots had been seriously hurt or killed when they landed in the middle of an unforgiving tree or were impaled on a snag or fencepost.

His aim was off a tad. He was clearly going to come down in a small stand of trees, and there would be no go-around for a second chance at landing. Then something about the situation seemed very familiar to him. Back home he, his brothers, and his friends often swung from pine sapling to pine sapling, high above the ground, like a bunch of monkeys. It was a convenient way to travel through the woods, and they sometimes did it for considerable distances.

Now, as he came down near a small tree, almost by intuition he reached over and got a good grip on its top branches. Sure enough, the twenty-foot-tall pine gently bent over toward the earth and gave him an easy ride the rest of the way down. It left him about a half foot above the ground. He simply stepped down onto solid dirt and let go of the tree. With a broad grin on his face, he stood there and allowed the parachute to settle down next to him. Brothers Roy and Hal Jr. and all their friends would have been proud of his rather elegant soft landing.

It was no time to celebrate still being alive, though. Every German in the area knew an American was down nearby. They would hurry to where he came in. Their goal was to find the downed pilot and capture him before he could find a good hiding place and make it more difficult for them to locate him. Or might be rescued by the locals—most of whom were not at all fond of the Germans—and be turned over to the French underground, the legendary Maquis Resistance fighters. Then the pilot might avoid being captured by the dreaded SS troops.

92

Captured pilots were highly prized by the Germans. The flyboys often knew much about what was going on with the war effort, including bits of information on the long-anticipated Allied invasion, pieces of a puzzle that could possibly be put together to create a picture of what to expect, when, and where. Pilots also knew the latest planned bombing targets as well, so defenses could be better placed and prepared. If the captive had had any interaction with the French Resistance, that information was especially prized. The Germans were very adept at obtaining that intelligence, too, regardless of the prisoner's intention not to cooperate. They were masters of interrogation, employing brutal torture if necessary.

Dragging his parachute behind him and limping on a leg that suddenly hurt very badly, Yeager made for the shadows of some larger trees about fifty feet away. It was dark in there. Dark and fragrant and even more painfully reminiscent of home.

But he could clearly hear the clanking of some kind of armored vehicle, probably a tank. And there were distant voices shouting in German. Yes, they knew he was there, and they had a pretty good idea of where he had floated down to the ground.

Now more recent training kicked in. During his time so far in England, he and the other pilots had undergone intense survival exercises, aimed at keeping them not only alive but also out of German custody. Yeager and the other pilots would be dropped off in a remote spot. Then they had to find their way to a designated place without being "captured" by elements of the British Army.

Now it was no longer a drill for Chuck Yeager. He kept

checking behind him, doing what he could to avoid leaving a trail. Despite the pain, he picked up and carried the heavy parachute rather than drag it through the pine needles and leave a track that someone could follow right to where he was hiding. He looked for blood, too. He was bleeding from several injuries, including a bad gash on his head from when he literally fell out of the cockpit of his upside-down airplane.

Later he would state that he probably walked through the woods four or five miles from the place where he had ridden the pine sapling down. When he could no longer hear any voices or vehicles and was confident he had a good hiding spot, he settled into a particularly tangled mass of thick brush. Then he pulled the chute in after him.

Time to take stock. He was now, he knew, officially "MIA." Missing in action. His folks back home would get the word. They would call Glennis and let her know, too. He hated to think about how much they all would miss him. How badly they would worry about him and wonder if he had survived at all.

The guys from his squadron at Leiston would drink shots and send up a prayer for him. The squadron losses had been minimal so far, but there had been some. And there was plenty of death all around with the other crews that had been penetrating deeply into Europe for a few weeks longer than the 363rd. While most of the men tried to ignore the carnage, it still bothered them. Especially when it was one of their own. Someone with whom they had spent the past year or so in training. Carousing with. Working and playing and drinking with.

Yeager treated his wounds as best he could, sprinkling sulfa powder on the places where shrapnel had peppered both feet, on a bad laceration on his right leg inflicted by a bigger hunk of flying metal, and on the nasty cut he got on his head when he bailed out. The bleeding had mostly stopped but he went ahead and bandaged each injury with gauze, mostly so he would not leave any sign on the ground or in the bushes that he had been there.

Next, he removed his jacket and, as best he could in the darkness of the deep shadows, considered the map of France that was sewn inside the lining of the leather flight jacket. He knew he was fifty miles east of Bordeaux, not far from the small German air base they had bombed just before the Focke-Wulfs showed up, swarming mad and ready to sting.

There was no way to know if there were friendly locals around or if this aromatic forest was held entirely by the Germans. And he certainly could not tell if there might be elements of the Maquis anywhere in the area. Luck might be the only determinant when he finally came face-to-face with someone who could be a friend or a foe. He would just have to be ready to react quickly should that luck turn out to be bad.

All Yeager knew was that he needed to get out of France as quickly as he could. Getting himself captured was not an option. He had his sidearm, a .45-caliber automatic. He would use it to defend himself. But he would also be certain to reserve one bullet, just in case that was his only option to avoid becoming a prisoner of war.

Even though he was cold and likely in shock from what he had just gone through, and even though his injuries hurt like hell—and despite the fact that he had a long way to go to get across the Pyrenees, through the winter snowpack, and into Spain, the closest "neutral" nation and the most likely way out—Chuck Yeager felt positive about his chances. He lay there in the brush and convinced himself that he would use his skills and determination to survive this mess in which he now found himself. He would get back to England. He would once again climb into the cockpit of another P-51, *Glamorous Glen II*, and he would get some revenge against the Luftwaffe for so sneakily ending his mission that day.

Well, maybe not the latter. The rules now stipulated that any Allied pilot unlucky enough to get shot down over France but fortunate enough to survive the ordeal and eventually make it back to England would not be allowed to fly combat missions over Europe again. There was a fear he might get shot down a second time, be captured by the Germans, and then be tortured into giving names of and information about the Maquis and others who had helped him during his previous rescue.

The policy now was that anyone who made it out alive after getting shot down would be shipped back home, likely spending the rest of the war in the States. He would either be mustered out of the service or assigned duty instructing other pilots or making the circuit selling war bonds, all the while explaining how he had gotten his ass blown out of the sky and lived to talk about it.

From the first hours after he parachuted into France from his destroyed Mustang, Chuck Yeager was already plotting how he would talk himself back into a P-51 and take it back to war. That became one of his goals once he decided he was, without question, going to make it out.

He had grown up in the woods. He could survive out there. He could hide from the Germans and the French who were sympathetic to the Nazis, get help from those who were not, and make it to Spain.

And he would fly combat missions again. He would help defeat Hitler. He would become an ace. He already had one kill. He needed only four more. He was confident he could achieve that in only another mission or two. Meanwhile, the pilot of every German plane he shot down would have the face of the man who blew *Glamorous Glen* out from under him over Bordeaux.

There was one other thing that made him feel better that first night as an "evadee," what the Army called a downed pilot on the run in enemy territory. While he was out here, hiding in the bushes, there would be no lucky Luftwaffe fighter pilot back at his base that night, celebrating with his buddies, enjoying slaps on the back and shots of whisky to commemorate his shooting down one of the enemy's best combat airplanes and its anonymous American pilot. No celebration for the German, like the one Yeager had enjoyed with his own comrades less than twenty-four hours before.

No, Yeager's wing mate had made certain that would not happen even as Yeager had slowly drifted down, totally at the mercy of gravity.

EIGHT

SLEEPING UNDER A PARACHUTE

No parts left. Just a smoldering hole.

—Chuck Yeager, describing in his official report the
condition of his P-51 Mustang (serial number 43-6763)
after having been shot down near Bordeaux, France

There had been no time to panic. When Yeager instinctively ducked and covered his face with his hands to try to avoid the bullets pocking his canopy, he knew his fighter had taken a big hit. And it was almost certainly done for. Then, when he raised his head again, he confirmed it. The Mustang's engine was on fire and a big chunk of one wing was gone. The plane was already out of control, starting to spiral downward.

Then, as he lay there on damp ground in the wooded darkness after having survived the attack, he tried to think of things he might have done to avoid the German pilot, to have kept from getting shot out of the sky, and to be able to spar with him. But the guy in the Fw 190 had simply gotten the jump on him. Yeager had been ambushed. If he had only seen the enemy plane a few seconds earlier, "tail-end Charlie" might have been able to dodge, duck, do a tight turn, put his Mustang through some gravity-defying maneuvers, and wreak his own violence on the Focke-Wulf.

But he had not. And now here he was, hiding like a wounded animal, hoping he could contact someone friendly. But he would do so with his pistol in his hand and ready to shoot if the first person he saw wore a German SS uniform. He was also already thinking about surviving, just in case he was going to have to do so for a while on his own.

He had no way to determine if the locals around these parts—mostly farmers and vineyard keepers—were sympathetic to the Germans or to the Allies. He did know from briefings how to determine whether they might be on the side of the occupation forces or not. Some of the French felt that the only protection for them and their families was to either kill or capture and turn over any downed pilots they might encounter. That was the only way to avoid suspicion that they might be guilty of harboring enemies of the Third Reich. The Germans knew each time when parachutes descended from an Allied bomber or fighter that had been shot down. If the survivor was not promptly turned in, dead or alive, the Germans were brutal in punishing the locals for not helping them find their prey.

On the other hand, Yeager knew, there were many who would risk everything to help get a pilot nursed back to health, sheltered, fed, and eventually transported out of occupied territory. That usually involved getting the pilot into the hands of the Maquis, who were very good at and dedicated to doing such things.

These members of the French Resistance were mostly young men who had rebelled against the Germans who had so boldly and brutally marched into their country. They also joined together and went underground to avoid the conscription of all able-bodied young males into the new Compulsory Work Service program created by their occupiers. In effect, they were to be forced to perform hard manual labor for the German military. Many of the men fled to the mountains, especially in southwest France and the Alps, and soon became an integral part of the French Resistance. One particular splinter group quickly developed into a very effective paramilitary organization, conducting deadly guerrilla warfare against the Germans. Others joined a secret army overseen by French military officers and conducted more organized operations. A third bunch fell into an even more formal militarized segment of the Resistance later in the war, serving as troops involved in conducting traditional forms of military attacks. The groups also formed along political lines as well, ranging from Communists to simple anti-fascists, but all aligned in their hatred for the Germans and their desire to end their occupation of France.

Some historians maintain that at its height as many as 400,000 men made up the Maquis. Their individual cells consisted of anywhere from a dozen or so members all the way up to hundreds. Not long after the German invasion of the country, their membership began to include more and more females, who fought right alongside the men.

The name Maquis came from the French word for bush or undergrowth. But the Germans had another word for not only the Maquis but all members of the Resistance. So did the fascist regimes in other countries nearby, including Spain. They called them terrorists. The government of unoccupied France—the

Vichy French—which continued to support and pledge loyalty to the German occupiers, bestowed the same term on their countrymen who dared to go underground and continue to fight back, often brutally and ferociously.

In addition to ambushing, sabotaging, and outright combat operations, an important role of the Maquis was to assist in escaping the country the downed Allied pilots, Jews, and any others being pursued by the Germans or the Vichy government. That usually required the help and cooperation of civilians who were not Resistance members.

That is where Chuck Yeager's timing was not the best. At about the same time he was shot down, in March of 1944, the German army had just begun a vicious campaign across France against anyone even suspected of assisting the "terrorists." This included many arrests, torture, and even mass slaughter, all of which were then well reported throughout the region so everyone would understand what would happen to them if they helped the Maquis.

There were two primary reasons for the ramp-up against the Resistance. First, their constant and very effective guerrilla tactics were taking a serious toll—in morale and in loss of equipment and personnel—on the German occupation troops. That included the success by the Maquis in shuttling pilots safely out of the country, thus denying the Germans the intelligence that could be tortured out of such valuable captives. And second, the Germans wanted to eliminate as much of the paramilitary threat as they could before the long-expected Allied invasion. That would allow them to better concentrate on repelling such an offensive without having to constantly watch their backs. The Resistance did not necessarily fight fair. Their methods could be grisly.

As it turned out, the Maquis did greatly assist the Allies during and after D-Day. They blew up railroads and bridges, attacked troop trains, and engaged in major battles with the Germans trying to fend off the Normandy invasion forces.

However, none of this was of concern to Chuck Yeager at the time. Not as he crawled deeper into the bushes, doctored his wounds, and hoped those SS soldiers who had seen him drift down into the pine tree would not be able to find him. He became aware that he was shivering. Probably from shock, he thought. But with his flight jacket off so he could study the map, and even though it was midafternoon on a mostly sunny day in March, it was cold there in the deep shadows of the forest.

Other members of his squadron had already been shot down in battle in the month they had been flying missions. Several were known to have been captured by the Germans. Yeager vowed to himself that he would not be a prisoner of war. That he would use those survival skills acquired playing kids' games and hunting squirrels and rabbits back home to sustain himself until he could get back to England. Then he would see what his future as a pilot looked like. And let his family know he had not augered in over there.

Several times before sundown, he heard low-flying aircraft overhead and assumed they were looking for him. And again there were distant shouts in German and the rumble of military vehicles of some kind. But nobody came near. He decided to wait there until it got dark. Then he would check the lay of the land while looking for fresh water and some food. He had seen fields about as he drifted down under his parachute. There were likely potatoes, carrots, or turnips already growing in the ground, even this early in the season.

However, once the sun was gone, a gentle rain began to fall. The clouds made it even darker. Too dark to forage for food or to determine if anyone he might meet wore an SS army uniform or not. He changed the plan. Yeager crawled beneath his parachute for cover, pushed aside some pinecones, sticks, and rocks, piled up some straw for a mattress, and, instead of fresh vegetables, settled for a tough, tasteless chocolate bar from his survival kit for dinner. As he dozed off, he decided rest was of some value, so he would not venture out into the chill, wet darkness after all. He would instead try to get some sleep and then emerge at first light. Surely the Germans would have given up looking for him by then, assuming he was either dead or had found assistance from a sympathetic local or the Resistance.

Sleep did not come easy. His wounds were painful, the ground was hard, and his stomach was growling from hunger. And he still tortured himself for having gotten himself shot down. It was difficult to take such failure only one day after realizing exhilarating success with his first actual air-to-air combat. He figured he was a better pilot than that.

Meanwhile, a third of a world away, near the Sierra Nevada Mountains, Glennis Dickhouse had no way of knowing about Chuck's situation. She would soon hear the bad news about him, though. As she continued her work at the USO, trying to make the lives of pilot trainees marginally better, she constantly kept in touch with Yeager by mail. She had continued to get letters from him as he prepared to ship out, then after he arrived in Great Britain and at Leiston, as heavily censored as they often were. She wrote him, too, almost every day. Even as his base changed, his mailing address remained the same. In his most recent letters, he had gone on at length about how exasperated he was becoming. He and the other pilots in his squadron seemed to always be "getting ready to start to commence to begin to think about" actually going to war and shooting down German planes. He was growing tired of all the training and still seeing so very little action in which he could help bring this war to an end.

When the letters abruptly stopped showing up in her mailbox about the middle of March, Glennis thought that he must have finally gotten what he had been wishing for. He was now likely to be flying missions where they would really count. And since he could not tell her much about what was going on once that became the case, she already expected that she would hear from him far less regularly now and for the rest of the war.

Then, one day toward the end of March, she got a phone call from Susie Yeager, Chuck's mother. The two women had never met or spoken with each other before. Glennis had not even known if the Yeagers had a telephone or, if they did, that they would know how to reach her way out there in Oroville, California. But Glennis realized at once that Mrs. Yeager making a long-distance telephone call meant she had something of great importance to tell her.

Glennis's heart skipped a beat. This was likely not to be good news.

The War Department had notified the Yeagers by telegram that Chuck was missing in action in occupied France. "Missing in action" made Glennis feel marginally better—as far as the Army Air Forces knew, he was alive—but that lasted only for a few moments. She heard enough talk among the pilots at the air base to know that getting shot down over enemy-occupied territory often meant the worst.

Then the very next thing Susie Yeager told her made her heart sing. Mrs. Yeager explained that the reason she was calling Glennis was because Chuck had written to his parents and told them that Glennis was the girl he was going to marry. "As soon as I get back home from the war, I am going to marry that girl," he had said in a recent letter.

"He had never told me that," Glennis would later say. But it was good to know. She felt the same about Chuck and had not really shared her true feelings with him, either.

Mrs. Yeager allowed that she was praying for her son and was certain God would get him through this ordeal and bring him back home safely. Glennis was not so sure. Around the USO, she had heard plenty of stories about the kinds of things that happened in battle, how often "MIA" became "KIA." Killed in action. She was realistic. Of course, she did not share those fears with Mrs. Yeager.

Even though she called the Yeagers weekly to ask if there had been any news, Glennis did not really expect much. The calls were more to try to make his parents feel better about his fate. "I didn't have much hope," she later admitted. "I figured Chuck was gone."

Though in a tight spot, Chuck Yeager was far from gone. In the dim predawn light, he awoke and stiffly crawled from the bushes where he had passed his first uncomfortable night in enemy-occupied France. His wounds and a few bumps and bruises he had not noticed the previous day now screamed at him. He tried to stretch out the kinks, then left his parachute behind as he pushed on through the thick, protective undergrowth and toward an open area near a plowed field. He kept his pistol in his hand, listening for any threatening sound.

Just as he reached the edge of the clearing and was about to step out into the open, he saw movement, someone walking in his direction along a narrow lane. It was a big man carrying an ax. One way or another, Yeager would have to determine if this man was friend or foe. The ax would not make that easy.

Yeager decided to wait for the man to pass by and then jump him from behind. He would first try to take that threatening ax away from him. Then, if he absolutely had to, he would use either it or the pistol to kill the man. The element of surprise gave Yeager the advantage. In seconds, the man lay there on the ground, clearly scared, and the ax had fallen well out of his reach.

Yeager pointed the barrel of his pistol directly at a spot between the man's wide eyes.

"American! Do you speak English?" Yeager asked the farmer. The Frenchman obviously did not. But he had heard "American." And likely could see that the man who had jumped him was in an American pilot's flight suit. The farmer slowly, cautiously put a finger to his lips to indicate *Be quiet.*

"Boches," the man whispered, moving his eyes left and right to indicate the enemy could be nearby.

"Boches" was a derogatory French word for German soldiers. That was a bit of information Yeager had gleaned from all the training in Britain. The word was a remnant of World War I, the "War to End All Wars." It can literally mean "rascal" or "cabbage head." There were likely enemy soldiers in the area, the farmer was trying to tell the American, so speak softly. He was also trying to make the point that he was no German sympathizer.

Yeager lowered his .45 and motioned for the farmer to stand up. Then, through gestures, the few French words he knew, and what little English the farmer could manage, and with a lot of facial contortions, he determined that the man would be willing to go find someone who spoke English. Someone who would be friendly and could help. He motioned for Yeager to get back into the bushes and hide there, that he would return soon.

Figuring he had little choice, Yeager did as the man suggested. He waited until the farmer—once again carrying his ax—was out of sight. Then he hid in the brush, but on the opposite side of the clearing. He kept his pistol handy, just in case. He had no way of knowing if the farmer would return with help or with a platoon of well-armed Germans. His only option then would be to take out as many of them as he could before they finished him off.

More than an hour passed before he heard footsteps—fast-moving footsteps—of at least two people coming his way. Yeager was not able to see them, but they stopped, talking quietly. They appeared to be looking into the woods at the point from which the pilot had first emerged to jump the farmer.

"I am a friend. You can come out."

The voice was heavily accented, but he spoke understandable English. Still, Yeager thought, it could be a fatal ruse.

"I am a friend. I can help you."

Yeager decided the odds were fifty/fifty. Maybe slightly better, since the farmer had returned not with a bunch of armed troops but with a single old codger with no sign of a weapon. Slowly he stood, pushed aside a few branches, and, with his handgun pointing directly at the backs of the two people standing there, emerged from his hiding spot into a patch of early-morning sun.

"You best be a friend," Yeager told the old man. "Or you're both dead."

The men turned slowly, hands up. Yeager had his finger ready to squeeze the trigger of his .45. Neither had a gun. Both smiled.

"I can help you, American pilot. *Oui?*"

"I'd be much obliged."

"Now what is your intent?"

Yeager told him he needed to get to somewhere neutral. That meant Sweden, Switzerland, or Spain. It was Yeager's understanding that any of these three countries would accept downed pilots or soldiers, but they would have to remain there until the war was over. Yeager did not have to think long about his options. Spain was easily the closest neutral country to where they now stood.

"Help me get to Spain," the pilot answered.

His newest best friend nodded and smiled.

"We can do our best."

The man introduced himself as a medical doctor. He took a quick look at Yeager's various wounds, saw nothing serious, and approved of the way the pilot had treated them already. Then they started walking.

For the first time in eighteen hours, Chuck Yeager now had full confidence he could and would get out of this mess and make it back to England. Then he kept telling himself throughout his journey that he would go aloft again and, by God, shoot down the son of a bitch who had ambushed him in the skies over Bordeaux.

NINE

"TRUST THEM"

*If you stick your neck out, you might get it bit . . . [I]t'll ruin
your whole day.*

—Chuck Yeager on *Late Night with David Letterman*,
September 10, 1982

S till wary, Chuck Yeager had no choice but to follow the
two men who had supposedly come to lead him to a place
of relative safety. They promised they would eventually
take him to people who could help, but it would be a difficult
journey. Germans were everywhere. Everyone was on alert for
downed Allied pilots. They would not be able to trust anyone
except those who were inside a very tight network, from French
people who hated Germany and its occupational forces all the
way to the storied French underground and the element of that
group known as the Maquis. The goal was to get Yeager to
Spain. He was correct in his belief that Spain, as a neutral nation and under the Geneva Convention guidelines, would have
to hold an Allied soldier, sailor, or pilot until the war was over.
Anything else would be a violation of those accords. The two
men who had come to his aid confirmed it. Still, Yeager believed
if he could get across those snow-covered mountains and into

Spain, he could find a way to get back to England and ultimately return to the war.

The trip to wherever they were taking Yeager took a while, since they were on foot and tried their best to stay near covering brush. Several times they jumped into the bushes when they heard voices or vehicles nearby. The three men finally reached a two-story stone farmhouse on the far side of a broad, grass-covered clearing. It would have been picturesque, idyllic, had it not been in the middle of German-occupied France. Just getting to the structure's front door meant they would be exposed and vulnerable. And if the two Frenchmen were leading him into an ambush, this would be the perfect spot for one.

Yeager still had no choice but to trust them. He followed the men across the clearing and then into the house, moving as quickly as he could, fully expecting to hear gunshots and shouting along the way. The older man led him straight through the farmhouse—Yeager did not see anyone else inside—out the back door, and then across another clearing and through the big open doors of a barn.

Inside, he was quickly amid the familiar aroma of hay, cow dung, and leather. Memories of home and Grandpa Yeager's farm washed over him. Then, with surprising dexterity for someone his age, the old fellow scurried up a ladder to the barn's second floor, which appeared to mostly be a hayloft. When Yeager hesitated, the man motioned impatiently for him to follow him up and then toward the back of the barn. There he opened a door to a small, dark, and dusty room.

The downed pilot hesitated. The old man gave him a surprisingly vigorous shove into the blackness.

Yeager heard a hasp close. He was now locked inside the room.

Next he heard the man hurriedly pitching hay against the door. From what little he had seen, it appeared he was in a storage room of some kind, with various tools hanging on hooks or stacked on the floor. But now, with the door closed and locked, it was dark, dusty, and very hot in there. It occurred to Yeager that he was now a prisoner.

There was a very good chance the old man—medical doctor or not—and the farmer with the ax had brought him there and hidden him in this rough cell so none of their neighbors could find and claim him as their own valuable prize. They would keep the money for themselves. The man who had been carrying the ax might already be on his way to fetch the Germans so they could collect the usual reward offered for downed Allied pilots and aircrew.

"Old-timer, am I being held prisoner in . . . ?"

"Quiet. The Germans. They are very near. You must be quiet or we are all in deadly trouble."

Sure enough, he now heard voices. German voices. They were outside, probably in the yard between the stone house and the big barn. Then they were closer, inside the barn, apparently asking the old man questions. And not doing so very politely.

Next, some of the soldiers were climbing the ladder to the hayloft. They seemed angry as they fussed with each other and rustled through the mounds of hay. It sounded as if they were stabbing into it with pitchforks. Yeager drew his .45 and aimed it at the door. He would not allow them to capture him alive if he could help it, and he was ready to take some of them with him before he died. He would not become a POW, certainly enduring torture and interrogation. No, he would go down fighting.

The German soldiers grunted, spat as they worked, and uttered what were probably curses, complaining about the heat and the dust, Yeager figured. The old man had clearly done a good job of covering the door of the little storage room with hay. They never probed anywhere near there. The soldiers soon climbed back down. It grew quiet. Maybe they had given up and left the barn. Or maybe not. Maybe they would threaten his rescuers, make them admit they had a pilot hidden away, intimidate them until they told them where they had concealed the American.

He could no longer hear them, but that meant nothing. The door was latched, so he could not escape anyway. There was nothing else to do but wait to see if the Germans came back and tried again to find him.

Hours passed. Yeager was half-asleep, covered in sweat, struggling to keep from coughing or sneezing from all the powdery dust, but with the pistol still clutched tightly in his aching right hand. Then he heard the creaking of the floor of the loft and footsteps coming his way. He forced himself to perk up, to lift the barrel of the gun and aim at the middle of the door, ready to shoot.

"Do not shoot, sir. It is I. The Germans have gone."

It was a good thing it was the old man. When he pulled open the door, even the weak light filtering into the loft was enough to temporarily blind Yeager after half a day in the darkness.

"Come," the man told him. "Follow me, please."

Yeager hesitated.

"Wait. How do I know you are not about to turn me over to those soldiers?"

The old man sighed, nodded, and reached into his coat pocket. He withdrew a note and handed it to Yeager. The words were handwritten in fancy script. And in English.

You are in safe hands, it read. *You can trust these men. Do as they tell you and they will help you escape.*

Yeager slowly stood but his legs did not seem to function properly. He even had a difficult time getting down the ladder to the ground. His injuries, although he did not believe them to be serious, were still painful enough to make it difficult to walk. He was stiff, too, from the uncomfortable closeness of the loft room. He was also dehydrated. But he trailed his rescuer out of the barn and into the farmhouse, where the old man motioned for Yeager to follow him up a set of stairs and to a bedroom on the second floor.

There, in the bed, lay an elderly woman covered in blankets, a heavy shawl draped over thin shoulders, and with an assortment of pill and medicine bottles on the nightstand next to her. But her eyes were noticeably strong and alert. She smiled slightly as she looked the American pilot up and down. He knew he was a pitiful sight, dirty, sweaty, and bloody.

"My, my, but you are so young," she told him, speaking in unaccented English. "Are the Allies so strapped that they now resort to having children fly their airplanes?"

"I'm no child," Yeager responded. "Most pilots are in their twenties. I'm twenty-one."

"Yes indeed. An old man." Her smile brightened. Then she

motioned for him to sit down in a chair near the bed and immediately began peppering him with questions. That accent of his? Where was he from? Was he married? If not, then why the ring on his right ring finger? The one where the French wore their wedding rings.

It was his class ring from Hamlin High School, Yeager told her.

The old lady finally seemed satisfied and offered an even warmer smile.

"I apologize for the interrogation," she said. "The Germans are now using imposters posing as downed pilots in an effort to catch those of us who dare assist the Allies. We must be sure you are legitimate, you know."

She explained that captured pilots or air crew were a prize when captured alive. They were taken off to be interrogated. But those who were helping them were summarily—and without the benefit of a trial—lined up and murdered, typically within view of their children, family members, and neighbors. That sent an obvious and strong message to others.

"We, though, have no love for the German occupiers," the woman told him. "Until they catch us and stop us, we will do what we can to help the Allies defeat Hitler. We—my husband and I—are too old to do much. But please be patient and we will connect you with others who will be able to help you. Trust them. But do exactly as they tell you, even if it makes no sense at the time. And perhaps, with luck, you will eventually return to West Virginia and find that young wife you deserve and have a houseful of children crawling about."

Yeager thanked her. Then the old man led him back down

the stairs to the kitchen. A young girl who had been hired to take care of the elderly lady upstairs had a delightful meal spread out on the table for him. Only then did Yeager realize just how hungry he was. It had been a day and a half since his bread-and-jam breakfast during the early-morning mission briefing back at Leiston. That seemed like weeks ago. Now he gobbled up the bread, cheese, and a delicious potato soup, all chased down by fresh milk with flecks of butter floating in it.

He later learned the lady was of Russian descent and had fled her native country during the revolution. She had been quite wealthy there but knew her wealth and ties to the existing government would have doomed her with Vladimir Lenin's socialist Bolsheviks. She and her husband brought with them as much money as they could and settled near Bordeaux. She felt Hitler's fascists were no better than Lenin's murderous socialists. Despite the risks, they were doing what they could to oppose the Germans.

"She was a cagey old gal," Yeager would later proclaim.

After breakfast, he returned to the hayloft storage room. This time the old man left the door unlocked but again took time to pile hay against it. And reminded Yeager that he must stay there and remain quiet, no matter what happened.

That order was soon to be tested. Although he had no idea the hour, it was sometime late in the evening when Yeager heard footsteps again, first on the ladder, then approaching. And again he pulled his .45 from his flight jacket, ready to blast away if the door was opened by men wearing SS uniforms.

It was a single man with a candle, his face obscured by the bright flame. In rough English he assured the pilot that he was a friend, also a doctor, and was there to look at his wounds. By candlelight, he carefully picked out bits of bloody shrapnel from Yeager's feet and hand. Then he inspected the gash in his calf. Apparently it had been caused by a larger piece of flying debris or possibly a bullet. It was not as deep as Yeager had feared. The doc put more sulfa powder on it and bandaged it up. Then, with a smile and a good-luck salute, the physician was gone. Yeager was once again all alone in his cramped, dusty, dark cell, with no idea how long he would be there.

As it happened, it was for a week. No soldiers ever came back to search the barn. There were only a few low-flying aircraft—no way to know if they were looking specifically for him—and that mostly stopped after a couple of days. The Germans had clearly lost interest in finding him, assumed he was dead, or figured someone would eventually see him trying to escape and report him for the reward money.

It was an intensely boring time for Chuck Yeager, who had always found something to do to occupy himself, wherever he was or whatever his situation happened to be. Not here. He had quit asking his hosts when they thought he might begin his journey toward Spain. They had no information for him. But soon, they promised. Sooner rather than later, they assured him. Yeager knew it was a trying time for them, too, always dreading the appearance of SS soldiers and the possible discovery of their hidden guest in the barn loft.

He volunteered to help the old couple with chores around their farm, but they refused his offer. He could not risk being seen by anyone. The farm, the smell of the earth, the chickens running loose in the barnyard—even the smell of the barnyard animals and the hay in the loft—made him powerfully home-sick for rural West Virginia.

So he sat and waited, mostly in the loft or far enough inside the open barn door that he could quickly disappear should he hear approaching troops or aircraft. He enjoyed the meals served to him in the farmhouse kitchen. Most of them were accompanied by delicious wine, which seemed as available as water in this place. The downtime allowed his wounds to heal up. He suspected there would be much walking and climbing ahead of him if he was to get to and over the Pyrenees. He made sure to pace around and around inside the barn during the day and hike the nearby open land surrounding the farmhouse by dark of night, all to stay in shape for the upcoming trek.

After nearly a week there, Yeager again asked his hosts when they thought he might be on his way. They remained vague.

"Just be ready to go with them," they always told him. "And trust them and do as they tell you."

"Not much I can do to get ready," he would remind them. He still wore his flight suit, the only clothes he had. And he was wearing them all the time. Even when he slept.

On his sixth night in the hayloft, Yeager had just dozed off when a rustle outside the door woke him. Instinctively, as he had done a few times when the old farmer or a rat made a noise, he pulled the gun and aimed at the door. The visitor had a candle. The SS would have come with flashlights and rifles. It was the doctor again, the one who had treated his wounds several nights before.

With a few English words but mostly exaggerated gestures, the doctor indicated that Yeager was to undress and put on the

Chuck Yeager during early flight training as part of the
US Army Air Corps' "flying sergeants" program.

Chuck Yeager in his P-51D Mustang fighter on the tarmac of
Royal Air Force Leiston, Great Britain, 1945.

Newly declared
as a fighter "ace,"
Yeager climbs into
the cockpit of
Glamorous Glen III.

An Army Air Forces bomber attack heavily damages a Focke-Wulf aircraft factory in Bremen, Germany, June 1944.

Chuck and Glennis Yeager at their wedding in Hamlin, West Virginia, February 26, 1945.

Captain Charles E. Yeager in 1948, just after becoming the first person to break the sound barrier.

Yeager stands next to one of the many planes he named after his wife, this one the Bell X-1 at Edwards Air Force Base in California.

Yeager in the cockpit of the Bell X-1 that he piloted through Mach 1 for the first time in history, October 14, 1947.

Parents Hal and Susie Mae Yeager with Chuck at the ceremony where he received the Harmon Trophy for aviation achievement.

Chuck and Glennis Yeager at another award ceremony where he was honored for becoming the first person to break the sound barrier.

Yeager at the dedication ceremony for the statue honoring him in his hometown of Hamlin, West Virginia, October 14, 1987.

Chuck Yeager retired from the Air Force on March 1, 1975, after a flying career that included active duty in three wars.

civilian clothes the man had brought him. Typical clothing worn by a French farmer or woodcutter. That included a black Basque-style beret that Yeager rather liked.

"*Expédition*," the doctor told him, motioning for him to follow him out of the barn. "How you say? Journey."

They walked in moonlight to thick bushes beyond the rear of the barn. There were two bicycles hidden there. There was an ax, too. The doctor handed it to Yeager and pantomimed using its strap and putting it on his back, carrying it as a woodcutter might. He also handed Yeager a leather pouch. He looked inside. There were forged identification documents.

"Germans? I talk. No you," the doctor instructed Yeager. Then the man nimbly climbed on one of the bikes. As he quickly pedaled away, he motioned for Yeager to get aboard the other one and follow, assuming the young American was even able to ride a bicycle.

Yeager was perfectly able, of course. Once he was moving through the cool night air, the young pilot was again filled with homesickness. He had ridden many miles on the country roads all around Lincoln County on various hand-me-down bicycles, some of which he had rebuilt himself. There was another irony that struck him as he pedaled away. He had been riding his bike that day when, as a kid, he went to see the crashed plane in the cornfield near the river. Now, in the direction they were going, they would likely pass near where his own fighter plane had so recently augered in to the French countryside.

Yeager was surprised when they just kept pushing on into the night. They pedaled in tandem for hours. At times he had to strain to keep up with the much older doctor. There was not much to see in the soft moonlight, so he made sure to keep close behind his tour guide so he could follow him wherever they were going. He also wanted to remain close in case they encountered German soldiers. He fully intended to heed the doc's caution, to stay quiet and let him do the talking. But he still kept his pistol within easy reach.

Yeager saw the first streaks of dawn on the horizon when the physician—not even breathing hard from pedaling up and down hills for most of the night—turned into a narrow lane that led to a small farmhouse. He motioned for Yeager to bring his bike around the house and into a barn. They put both bicycles on the ground and quickly covered them with straw, then each settled into empty stalls. There they made the best bed they could and proceeded to sleep for most of the day. After the long night's pedaling, Yeager easily found sleep.

No one bothered them. As soon as the sun was down the next day, they ate food someone had left nearby the night they had arrived, then uncovered their bikes and pedaled away into the darkness. It was the same deal the next morning, but the inhabitants of the next farm fed them well upon arrival. Then both Yeager and the doctor went upstairs and spent that day soundly sleeping on real feather beds.

The two men spent most of their time moving, stopping only to relieve themselves in the bushes, drink from a waterskin the doctor had, and rest a few minutes before hurrying on. There was little time for talk, and the language barrier prevented any meaningful conversation anyway. But near dawn on the second night of the brutal journey, the doctor stopped at a crossroads and pointed to a direction sign.

One arrow pointed to a town named Roquefort. Yeager recognized it. The cheese, of course. The other indicated that the road that led off in the opposite direction went to a place named Nérac. The doc pointed that way and pedaled off. Yeager followed.

It was still dark when they rolled silently into the yard of another farmhouse. Again they hid the bicycles in the nearby barn before knocking at the back entrance to the house. They were greeted by a burly man with a black mustache who motioned for them to come in. He cautiously looked all around outside, making sure no one had seen his early-morning visitors.

The two Frenchmen embraced, then shook hands. With a nod to Yeager and a quick *"Au revoir,"* the doctor pulled on his hat and went back out the door.

"Merci," Yeager told him. He had spent hours riding along with the man, they had eaten and slept within feet of each other for two nights, but they had probably not exchanged more than a few awkward words. He did not even know the doctor's name. The last time Yeager saw him, he was rolling out of the barn, down the lane, and back off in the direction from which they had just come.

"He is a good man," the farmer told him, nodding solemnly and speaking passably good English. "I am Gabriel. My wife will have food soon. Then we have a place for you to hide until we turn you over to your next rescuers."

Over breakfast, the two men shared conversation, including details of Yeager's upbringing and how he had managed to become a pilot without the usual academic requirements. Gabriel seemed especially interested in the jobs Yeager had held as a boy and particularly those he did with his father in the coal mine gas fields. They lingered over breakfast much later than they intended, until the sun was well up in the blue sky, but the man seemed generally intrigued by Yeager's story. And the young pilot was more than happy to finally have someone he could talk to. The coffee was delicious, too.

This farmhouse was located very near a busy roadway. German military vehicles had passed by already but none of them had even slowed. Even so, Gabriel had many questions on one particular subject: Yeager's experiences with explosives. And he freely offered details of what he had done to help his dad.

Finally, the big farmer stood and told Yeager to finish his coffee, then follow him.

"You will be safe in the shed here for a few days," he said. "There is no hurry. We must wait for the snows to melt some more in the mountains that separate France and Spain. You would not be able to make it across on foot until then."

"How long will it be?" Yeager wondered aloud. He had hoped to already be in Spain by now. From there, he should be able to get word out about his fate. If they had not already, his folks, his brothers and sister, and of course Glennis would soon learn that he was missing in action. As time passed, they would assume he had been killed in action. He needed to tell them differently.

"We will know the right time," Gabriel told him. "You must trust us and do as we say. You will be in hiding with the next rescuers until the time is right to give you a better chance to safely return to your base." He opened the back door and cautiously looked around. "But I believe your next stop will offer a much more interesting time than you will spend here hiding in my shed. You see, Flight Officer Yeager, you have some skills that will be of great value to those who fight against the Nazis."

Yeager had only a quick opportunity to give Gabriel a puzzled look before the big man was out the door and briskly trotting toward a small structure mostly hidden in a clump of thick bramble bushes at the far side of the yard.

Yeager shrugged and, as he had been doing for almost two weeks now, followed this total stranger to the next dusty, dark, dangerous hiding place.

TEN

FUSE MAN FOR THE MAQUIS

I'm put in charge of the explosive fuse devices. I . . . show
Robert how to set them for different timings . . . And that
will be my assignment for as long as I'm with these guys:
Maquis fuse man.

    —Chuck Yeager, in *Yeager: An Autobiography*

It did not take long for Yeager to determine that he had now met his first full-fledged Maquis member. Only later did he find out that Gabriel—he never did learn his full name— was not only a member but the regional chief of the underground group. He also learned that the man with whom he had been bicycling through the south of France was Dr. Henri, and he served as the physician for all the Maquis in the area. Yeager felt honored that such a man had tweezered shrapnel from his feet and hands.

For now, though, all he knew for sure was that he was hiding out in Gabriel's toolshed, listening to German vehicles rush past on the little country road and waiting for the snow to melt in the mountains.

He did occasionally take meals with Gabriel's family. That included his wife, Marie Rose, their son, Marie's brother, Léon, and Gabriel's mother. The women were good cooks, which meant excellent meals. Little wonder Gabriel was such a big man. And Gabriel was a talker, too, and that made for good conversation as entertainment. None of the others spoke any English, except for the one phrase Marie Rose repeated over and over as she dipped out food for Yeager: "We love Americans."

Still, Yeager mostly just hunkered down in the shed and only came out for fresh air under a late-night, star-filled sky. Occasionally he kicked a ball around with Gabriel's son in a field behind the shed. One day Yeager decided to get some sun for a few precious minutes, sitting in the grass and leaning against a fence post not far from the road. He must have dozed and was suddenly awakened by a large contingent of German soldiers marching past, raising clouds of dust.

He did not panic. He remained still, hoping they would not notice him. And if they did, that they would assume he was nothing more than a farmhand taking a break from raking hay. If he jumped up and ran, it would surely raise suspicions. He still had his .45 in his pocket. Although he would have had no chance against all those Nazi soldiers, he would have done whatever he could to take out some of them before they finished him off.

They apparently did not see him. Or if they did, they were not at all curious. But somebody else did see the extremely close call.

As soon as the Germans were out of sight, Gabriel was at the back doorway of the house, hissing angrily, waving for Yeager to hurry over.

"Stay in the shed!" Gabriel told him. "If they see you, it will be over for you. For me. And over for my family."

Yeager apologized sincerely and crawled back into his hiding place.

One moonless night, well after sundown, just as he was drifting off to sleep, Yeager heard a knock on the door of the toolshed.

"Come with me, Flight Officer Yeager." It was Gabriel. "Bring your possessions."

Yeager had no bags. Or clothes, other than the ones he wore. He only had to pull on his beret and the civilian coat he had been given and he was ready.

It seemed much longer, but it had only been a little over two weeks since he had been shot down. Now it felt good to finally be going somewhere. Anywhere. His wounds had healed, and the night air was fragrant with the aroma of pine trees. But he had no idea that this night hike would end up taking most of two days to complete.

By daylight, they had pushed deeply into the thick forestland. They stopped and shared food and water that Marie Rose had prepared for them. Then they were moving again, mostly uphill, and with no signs of any other human beings, cultivation, or habitation. Near dawn at the end of the second night, Gabriel stopped and turned to Yeager.

"You will wait here," the big man said. "I will go on from here alone. I will be back for you."

Then he was gone, lost in the thick woods.

Yeager found a decent hiding place in the brush and ate the last of the food Gabriel had brought. There he waited for the rest of the day. He began to worry that something had happened to Gabriel. That maybe he had sent some of the Maquis to get him and they could not find the right spot. But then common sense took over. The underground fighters would likely not reveal themselves in full daylight, even in this remote and heavily forested area. They would come at night.

That was exactly how it happened. It had been dark about an hour before he sensed more than heard the men approaching.

"American. It is Gabriel. It is safe to come out."

It was difficult to tell how many of them there were. They wore dark clothing and berets, and their chests were crossed by bandoliers full of bullets. These were the Maquis, the French underground, and they clearly meant business.

"You will stay with these men until the snow is not so deep so you have more of a chance to cross into Spain," Gabriel told him. "You can trust these men. Do as they tell you. I also believe you will be able to help them in their mission."

Gabriel flashed a salute and walked back into the blackness of the forest.

The group's apparent leader introduced himself as "Robert." He spoke very good English, but the others either did not or simply felt it best not to talk. As they all hiked on, Yeager counted about two dozen of them. He learned that Robert was an attorney from a town not far from where they now walked. He had been with the Resistance for over two years. He had long since stopped going home regularly to see his family. The Germans knew who he was. He now hid in the mountains, sleeping and eating during the day, then emerging at night to go down to harass German patrols and bivouacs, blow up trains, and take out critical bridges. They hoped their efforts would make it easier for the Allies when and if they invaded France and began to push toward Berlin.

They seemed disappointed when Yeager told them he knew little to nothing about any potential invasion. But, he assured them, America would one day help liberate France, and he was convinced it would be soon. That answer pleased his rescuers.

It soon became obvious that these men knew these woods well. Robert assured him that all the members of his group were from the area and that they were dedicated to one thing: killing Germans. But Yeager should be prepared to move camps often. They rarely remained in a place for more than one night.

Robert also told Yeager that the Germans had a primary goal: to find and kill the Maquis. The SS were constantly searching for them, usually by air, employing their Fieseler Fi 156 Storch (Stork) aircraft. Those small, single-engine planes were primarily designed for battlefield surveillance, but their very low stall speed of about 31 miles per hour made them quite effective for searching the mountains and forests for any sign of the French Resistance fighters.

Yeager asked Robert why they did not just use their weapons to try to shoot down the Storks. The guerrilla fighter merely smiled and said, "Whether we hit or miss, the Germans would bomb the whole area within a quarter hour."

That meant the Maquis had to be on the move constantly. And Chuck Yeager had to be on the move with them. They typically camped twice per day, securing food and supplies from caches hidden throughout the area by sympathetic locals. Then, when it was dark, they crept down to do their sabotage work. At times their mission was to assassinate someone they had determined was an informer. There were many who pretended to be loyal to the Maquis but were actually telling the Germans everything they could learn about who was a part of the Resistance, where they hid, what mischief they would unleash next, or who else was helping them in their cause.

"One of my own cadre members could be a double agent, you know," Robert told him as they sat and ate in near total darkness. Yeager was glad he could not see the faces of the men with whom he now trusted his own life.

For the first few nights, the group left Yeager behind while they went out to do what they did. Often they were operating on information from spies who worked in places such as railroad yards or those who supplied the SS troops with gasoline or fresh food. But Yeager remained at the last camping spot, usually with a very old man who served as cook and a couple of younger members designated to guard the camp.

At one point he helped butcher a cow the Maquis had "requisitioned" from some farm in the area. The cook and young guards seemed impressed with the American pilot's expertise. Perhaps this was the unique skill that Robert had spoken about that made this particular downed pilot so valuable to the Maquis. But it was only another example of knowledge acquired growing up in the West Virginia mountains and spending so much time on Grandpa Yeager's farm.

After a few nights with the Resistance fighters, Robert invited Yeager to go with them to retrieve materials that would be dropped from a Royal Air Force plane. After about a four-hour walk, they finally reached their spot. Even then, they had to wait another hour or so, well past midnight on a chilly night, before they heard approaching aircraft engines. Yeager knew at once what kind of bird it was: an RAF Avro Lancaster heavy bomber. The grumble of its four Rolls-Royce Merlin engines was unmistakable. His now-deceased P-51 had been powered by one of those very same engines.

As one of the Maquis signaled with his flashlight, the Lancaster flew over on a frighteningly low pass, barely treetop high. Then the big plane banked and made a second run overhead, this time dropping a big container with two parachutes billowing out above it. As the bomber flew off into the overcast, the Maquis rushed out to greet the freight as it settled into a small clearing.

Then, to Yeager's considerable surprise, two oxen emerged from the trees pulling a cart. The men quickly hoisted the container onto the cart, and it disappeared back into the shadows of the tall pines. From the time the Lancaster's engines became audible until the oxcart was lost in the night, less than five minutes had elapsed.

"I never could figure out how the Maquis communicated with the British to arrange those air drops," Yeager later commented. And the underground fighters certainly were not going to share those details with anybody.

Later, Yeager found himself with Robert and his crew in a dimly lit barn, breaking out the contents of the big shipping container. It seemed obvious why some of the items were included. There were a number of the lightweight and very effective British Sten submachine guns. Spanish-made Llama

.38-caliber pistols. Ammunition for those weapons. But some of it surprised Yeager. There were scores of neatly wrapped packages of counterfeit franc notes. And counterfeit ration stamps. But those items made eminent good sense once he thought about it.

Then, near the bottom of the container, he spied some items that looked very familiar to him. There were big packages of plastic explosives. Fuses. Timing devices. He had certainly seen plenty of those items before. They were even American made and the very same types he had worked with when he helped his dad tap, pump out, and capture the underground pockets of natural gas around the coal mines back in the Appalachians.

Most of the men spread out from the barn to hide the cache of weapons and ammunition in other barns, cellars, toolsheds, and haystacks. Robert and Chuck headed on back to the last encampment. There, Yeager showed the Maquis leader how to best handle the plastic demolition materials, how to set the fuse for different time increments, how much to use depending on the target and amount of damage desired, how not to waste a bit of it, and more. This was valuable information. They had been doing the best they could but not achieved the results they wanted. Robert knew Yeager's expertise would greatly increase the effectiveness of his crew. By the time the sun came up, Chuck Yeager, fighter pilot, had become Chuck Yeager, Maquis fuse man.

Until the snow would allow passage over the high mountains at the French and Spanish border, Yeager's job would be to cut up chunks of plastique explosives of the proper size to destroy whatever the target was and to attach the explosives to a fuse that would allow adequate and predictable time for the saboteurs to get away and for the blast to happen at the precise time desired.

It came easy to him. Even though Yeager had been taught in training that combatants of one country should not aid in any way guerrilla fighters in another, he felt it was his duty. His way of paying back the Resistance fighters who were further risking their own lives to get him safely out of the country.

Yeager would later note his amazement that the Germans were never able to infiltrate the Resistance in France. Part of the reason was that there were simply too many of the Resistance members. But a big factor was that so many of the French resented the invasion of their homeland by Hitler's forces. Despite bribes and bounties, most were more than willing to help the Maquis and other factions of the underground, whether it was fighting with them, feeding and sheltering them, or simply keeping quiet about them.

Doing what he could do for the effort gave Chuck Yeager the satisfaction of knowing he was helping to shorten—and win—this nasty war. And blowing up a bunch of German soldiers in the process.

ELEVEN

THE PYRENEES

It is dark in the back of the lorry and my companion does not speak English, but I know this is it. We are going south, toward the Pyrenees.

— Chuck Yeager, describing the start of the final leg of his journey from occupied France to Spain

It was a wet and cold afternoon, the twenty-second of March, a Wednesday. Yeager had slept most of the day after a busy night cutting up plastique and inserting timing fuses. Several of the Maquis were preparing to slip into Nérac to buy medicine, food, and cigarettes, using the counterfeit ration coupons and money from the recent RAF drop. It was possibly their most dangerous job. The town was full of Germans, Vichy French police, and plenty of others not so easily identified as enemies. There were rumors that a major force of SS troops had been moved into the area, and another that the Germans and forced laborers were constructing a medical facility in the little farming town big enough to accommodate more than seven hundred wounded men. Clearly, Hitler and his army were preparing for an Allied invasion as soon as the weather permitted it.

Yeager had just sat down with a bowl of stew when Robert, the Maquis leader, tapped him on the shoulder and motioned for him to step outside with him.

"You are going into town with those two men," Robert told him, pointing to a pair of Resistance fighters standing a short distance away. With a grin, the Maquis leader added, "Just stay with them and you will be okay."

Yeager started to object. Too much could go wrong in town. He was relatively safe there in the mountain hideout. No reason for him to take such a risk. But Robert abruptly turned and went back into the barn. And the two men began walking off into the misty darkness, assuming he would follow them. Yeager shrugged and ran to catch up.

It was soon apparent that they were not headed toward town at all. After only a few miles, they came upon a narrow country lane. There was a van or lorry parked there, its headlights off. The sign on its side said it was from the Crayons Franbel Entreprise. The Franbel Pencil Company, a local manufacturer of writing instruments.

As the three men approached, the back door abruptly swung open. Yeager stopped, ready to bolt. But a young man motioned for him to get inside and offered him a hand. Once the door closed behind him, the inside of the van was completely dark. He had to quickly find a seat on the floor and grab something solid for support, because they were immediately in motion.

He sensed there was no one else inside the lorry besides the man who had helped him inside, but it was really too dark to see for sure. Apparently his fellow passenger spoke no English, either. But it was clear to Yeager what this was. The time had come for him to attempt the final leg of his journey into Spain.

As best he could tell, they traveled over rough road and at a good speed for more than two hours before suddenly coming to a hard stop. They waited a bit, remaining quiet. Then the door of the van was pulled open from the outside and a man in dark clothes animatedly beckoned Yeager to get out and follow him.

They had parked close to a high wall, apparently in a small village. He followed the man around the corner, where another van sat in the dark drizzle, its engine idling. When the rear door opened, Yeager got a glimpse of several other men inside, seated on benches on either side of the vehicle. When the door closed, though, he was once again engulfed by darkness. Nobody spoke. The truck immediately took off and was soon racing around sharp turns, braking hard, then resuming its breakneck speed. Yeager—and he assumed the others, whom he thought were probably Allied bomber crew members or fighter pilots—held on as best he could. He could only hope the trip would not be this rough all the way to Spain.

Then, finally, the van slowed. It was apparent that they were climbing. The driver constantly worked up and down through the gears.

After a bit, a flashlight illuminated the interior of the van and a Frenchman who had been seated at the end of one of the benches eased over to a spot in the middle where the others could see and hear him over the strain of the van's engine. Yeager could now confirm that there were three other escapees making the dangerous trek with him.

The Frenchman informed them that they were now approaching the city of Lourdes in the foothills of the Pyrenees. Then he gave each man a rough hand-drawn map and explained that it showed several possible routes they could follow. The man told them they could hike together or separately but suggested they at least pair up and not try to go it alone. This particular time for their evacuation had been chosen because the weather had recently been relatively mild in the mountains. The typical four feet of snow had likely melted some. There should be no blizzards over the next four or five days, either. That was about how long it would take for them to make the trip on foot. Assuming, of course, that they were not intercepted by enemy patrols.

Then the man offered a somber warning. The routes were heavily patrolled by German troops looking specifically for Allied military evacuees on the run but also for smugglers and refugees fleeing occupied France. Even if they made it to Spain—where the country was officially neutral in the war but decidedly fascist politically—there was always the possibility that some elements of the military there, or even civilians, would capture them and turn them in to the SS. Should they be captured, they should not assume that the Geneva Convention rules would protect them in the least. The Germans would torture them for information, including details on how and by whom they had been smuggled out of France.

After, of course, they would be executed.

When the vehicle finally skidded to a rough stop and the Frenchman opened the back door of the van, the men inside could see they were on a rudimentary logging road surrounded by trees and brush. The Frenchman pointed toward a rough woodsman's hut amid the undergrowth and suggested they rest there, stay warm and dry, and await daylight. It was probably three or four hours before sunrise and a light rain was falling. It would be dangerous to proceed through such terrain in the dark.

The Frenchman handed each escapee a big knapsack, wished them all good fortune, then climbed into the front of the van with the driver, and they were gone, quickly lost in the damp darkness and mist.

The four airmen followed the Frenchman's advice and sought shelter in the hut. Then, at first light, they decided to slog along together. The going quickly became very difficult. They were up to their knees in slushy snow, and although there was a rough trail, it mostly involved climbing. The footing made that a challenge. So did brush, fallen trees, and boulders.

Yeager's first impression once it was daylight was that the Pyrenees looked very much like the Sierra Nevada Mountains. He had become very familiar with them while he was in the area during his days in pilot training. They reminded him of Glennis, too. She had grown up in the foothills of the Sierras. Chuck had hunted and fished in those mountains as well. But never with three or four feet of wet snow to slog through to get to a good fishing hole.

By midday of their first day of the crossing, Yeager and one of his traveling companions had pushed well ahead of the other two evaders. The man was Omar M. "Pat" Patterson, a navigator on a B-24 Liberator. He had been shot out of the sky somewhere over France. When they reached a spot just above the tree line, they decided to stop, rest, eat, and wait for the other two men to catch up. The knapsacks contained food, dry socks, medicine, money, and other items they might need along the way.

But after an hour, and with no sign of the others, Yeager and Patterson decided to push on. They hoped to make good progress the first day and find shelter in another logger's hut for the night. There was one indicated on the map, and reaching it was a reasonable goal.

The going became even more difficult. At times they had to sit down and slide along on the ice to make progress. They had no idea what elevation they might have reached by then. The peaks were higher than 11,000 feet, but the rough map supposedly showed passes that were lower. Still, the air had grown very thin. It was difficult to breathe, and the lack of oxygen made them weak and dizzy. Soon their necessary rest stops became more and more frequent and lasted longer and longer before they felt up to pressing on.

There was still no sign of the other two airmen, either. Yeager felt guilty about that, but there was nothing he could do.

They were not able to make it to the cabin before darkness fell. Patterson and Yeager ended up spending the first night beneath a rock outcropping, trying to avoid a bitter wind and flakes of snow. The next two days were no better. The hike was extreme. They had not yet spotted any other structure, so they still had to shelter among the rocks, covered by pine boughs and little else. The weather was terrible. Their boots leaked, so they wore two of the four pairs of socks in their knapsacks at a time to try to keep their feet dry and warm. Frostbite was a real worry.

Most of the time the fog limited visibility to thirty or forty feet. What little sun they saw through the heavy overcast was still in the expected place in the sky, confirming they were going in the correct direction. They had no reason to believe they were lost. But by this time they felt they should have been on the downslope. They should be seeing some of the landmarks indicated on the maps the Frenchman had given them. Those would confirm that they were near the Spanish border.

The other two men still had not caught up. Were Yeager and Patterson on the wrong course while the others were already entering Spain?

Night was quickly approaching on their fourth day of foot travel. The two men had just climbed a steep ridge and were struggling for breath. Neither could feel his legs from the waist down. That was when they almost stumbled into the front doorway of a logger's hut that was indicated on the map. They were very near the border. And the hut might just as well have been a four-star hotel!

Still aware of the danger, both men drew their handguns as they carefully pushed open the door of the cabin. Nobody was there. They collapsed inside, pulled off their socks and wrapped themselves in the blankets from their knapsacks. Patterson hung his two pairs of socks to dry on the limbs of a bush just outside the door. Yeager laid his out on the cabin floor. Then they pulled on dry socks and their boots to try to warm up their feet.

Of course, they dared not try to start a fire. The smoke would have attracted plenty of attention. Even so, compared to being outside in the icy wind, the place seemed almost warm and welcoming. Before they could even break out bread and cheese from their knapsacks, both men fell into a deep sleep, lying side by side there on the rough cabin floor.

They were still sleeping at dawn when they were awakened by all hell breaking loose. Rifle fire from outside. Bullets hitting all around them. Bullets coming through the walls and the half-open front door. Only later would Yeager deduce that a passing German patrol had spotted Patterson's socks drying on the bush outside the cabin. The SS troops asked no questions. They simply opened fire.

Both men did the only thing they knew to do. Yeager grabbed his knapsack and they jumped out the small rear window of the cabin into the deep snow. Patterson screamed. He had been hit in the leg. Yeager helped him up and supported him as best he could as he looked for any available route of escape. They could not stop or try to hide. That would mean capture, and that was not an option.

Then Yeager spotted a log flume not thirty yards away. Filled with snow, it meandered down the steep back side of the ridge. It was a long trough, similar to the ones he was familiar with from back home, used by lumbermen to slide logs downhill to a river so they could be floated to the nearest sawmill. Just then, with German soldiers peppering the cabin with bullets, it was their only available escape route. He did not hesitate. He shoved Patterson down the flume, then jumped into it himself.

The wild ride down probably took only a few seconds, but it

seemed like hours of twisting and turning before the flume ejected Yeager into thin air and he fell into an icy-cold creek. If the SS bullets had not awakened him, the brutally cold water certainly did. He popped to the surface at the same time as Patterson. But his companion did not look good. He had taken a bullet to his right knee and was losing lots of blood.

Yeager summoned up all the strength he could find and swam with one arm while holding Patterson's head above water and pulling him toward the far bank, even as the swift water carried both of them farther downstream. He could still hear the rifles firing up there on the top of the ridge, the Germans not relenting, ripping apart their accommodations for the night. But the shooting was now growing more distant as the cold water transported them away.

When they reached calmer water, Yeager pulled Patterson out of the stream and onto the bank. He was shocked by what he saw. The bullet—likely some kind of expanding or exploding round—had hit the navigator's knee, almost severing the limb. Only a tendon held the leg on. The icy-cold water had slowed the bleeding somewhat, but it had already started up again.

Yeager knew what he had to do. He grabbed a small knife from his knapsack. He cut the tendon, effectively amputating Patterson's leg. Then he used some clothing from the knapsack—including a shirt one of his hosts had made from parachute fragments—to fashion a bandage for the stump and a tourniquet to wrap around Patterson's thigh. That hopefully would stop the bleeding. If it did not, Patterson would not last long at all.

Yeager considered their options. Only one made any sense. He would have to wait until dark and then try to climb the next ridge while carrying or dragging the lieutenant, who was now unconscious but breathing. From there, and according to the hand-drawn map, they should finally be able to see Spain. It would be downhill from there.

The effort was far more than Yeager even imagined. Pulling the deadweight of Patterson made it far more than twice as difficult. At times he slipped on the ice-encrusted snow and slid all the way back down the mountainside, pounding hard into rocks and trees along the way, negating several hours of taxing progress. But somehow he managed to get a grip on Patterson, made sure he was still breathing, and stubbornly climbed right back up. Later, Yeager would admit that he could not remember much of the torturous effort. Nor could he affirm what made him keep going, not once considering letting go of Patterson and leaving him behind. That would have offered much better odds for Yeager to get himself out of that mess. But the navigator would not have lasted the day out there.

Yeager would eventually decide that it was just that damned work ethic instilled in him by his dad and by Grandpa Yeager. You left no job undone. You finished what you started. And you did it the best you could.

Sometime during the night, he had simply gone as far as he could go, tugging Patterson along with him, using a pine limb as a sled. And at that point he settled down for a quick rest. There he passed out.

A brilliant burst of rare sunlight awakened him. The first thing he did was check on Patterson. The lieutenant was still breathing. Surprisingly regular breathing. His face was gray, but somehow he was still alive. Yeager realized that they were, remarkably, at the crest of the ridge. When he stood and walked over to the southwestern edge of the bluff, he spotted the road they were supposed to be looking for, just on the Spanish side of the border. Now, all he needed to do was figure out how he was going to get down there. And even more problematic: get his friend down to the road, too. It was not far away at all but mostly a sheer drop, cut by a ravine that led down to a spot near the roadway.

Yeager grinned. He recalled all the times he and his brothers and friends played in the snow in the mountains around Hamlin. One of their favorite activities had been ripping limbs off pine trees and using them as sleds as they rode down gullies and draws, all the way to the bottom. The best tree limbs offered the ability to lean backward or sideways to steer and brake themselves along the ride down. If that failed, they could always dig in their heels and try to slow down. Sometimes it worked. Sometimes they wrapped themselves and their rough sled around a boulder or a pine at the bottom of the gulley.

Now he found a good limb, dragged Patterson onto it, and then pulled him over to the top of the long, straight draw that ended near the roadway. *Hell of a way to visit Spain*, Yeager thought as he shoved the limb and the navigator over the side. Then he watched as Patterson rode, still unconscious and totally unaware, all the way down. It turned out to be a relatively uneventful journey for the bomber navigator.

Then Yeager found his own branch, hopped aboard, and followed Patterson's route downward. He ended up very close to Patterson. He still had to give his partner a few more short rides down the icy slope before they finally reached the roadway. The

Frenchman in the back of the van had told them this road would be heavily patrolled by the Spanish Guardia Civil, one of the country's law enforcement agencies. They would be most likely to help the American evadees. Few others they might encounter on the road would.

Yeager made certain that the lieutenant could easily be seen from the road, made him as comfortable as he could—he now appeared to be on the verge of death—whispered, "Good luck," and then walked off down the road in the direction indicated by an arrow on the hand-drawn map.

He would later learn that Patterson had been picked up by a Guardia Civil patrol less than an hour after Yeager left him. He was still alive. Once he received medical attention, the B-24 crewman would be back in England within six weeks. Pat Patterson's war was over but not his life, thanks to the persistence and work ethic of Chuck Yeager.

It was almost dusk by the time Yeager walked into a small village, dog-tired and cold. Without hesitation he headed straight for the local police station. He did not want to be taken for a smuggler and get himself shot to death before he could identify himself. Not after all he had just been through to reach this little burg. Best to go right to the authorities and let them help him find accommodations for the night. They could also put him in touch with the proper authorities to arrange his return to England.

Once there, he could begin lobbying to be allowed to return to the skies and shoot down Germans. He had been formulating in his head the arguments he would make as he and Patterson made their arduous journey across the mountains. That was one thing that kept him putting one foot in front of the other.

But things did not go at all as he had expected.

Before the night was over, Chuck Yeager would find himself locked up and required to stage a jailbreak.

Then, before the next day was finished, he would enjoy chicken and beans and a two-hour bath.

Ultimately, he would sleep a solid two days before taking the next step in the process of getting back into the cockpit of a Mustang and returning to the war.

TWELVE

THUMBS-UP

They started publishing orders for me to go back to the United States. I told them I did not want to go home. I wanted to go back and fight. I only made eight missions. They said I couldn't. The rules prohibit it.

—From an interview with Chuck Yeager,
Academy of Achievement, Cedar Ridge,
California, February 1, 1991

T he police in the town of Lérida, Spain, were hardly accommodating when the man claiming to be a downed American pilot stumbled into their headquarters. There was good reason. The Germans had begun sending spies out, pretending to be Allied pilots. Spain was supposed to be neutral and thus not giving aid to enemies of the Third Reich. Even though this one appeared to have made a long journey on foot—he was dirty, had blood on his clothes, and was wet from the snow and blue from the cold—they shoved the new arrival right into a nearby jail cell and locked the door. The police would attempt to confirm his story the next day as well as check with higher-ups on what to do with this man claiming to be an American fighter pilot. Meanwhile, he would have to remain in the cell.

Chuck Yeager objected as vociferously as he dared. All he wanted was to check in with the authorities and get a recommendation for a place to find warmth, some rest, and a meal. None of the policemen spoke English nor did they appear to be in any mood for a debate. After locking him securely in the cell, he was left alone, apparently for the night, with no food, water, or dry clothes.

Once he was satisfied they were gone and no one was likely to be coming back, Yeager pulled from his inside coat pocket his pilot's survival kit. Thankfully, the police had been in a hurry to go home for supper. They had not bothered to search him. In that kit was a small but very rugged saw blade designed specifically for use by pilots to extricate themselves should they find themselves locked up in a jail cell. The blade worked nicely on the brass bars that stood between Yeager and food, a bath, and a bed.

Once outside the police station, it was not far at all to a boardinghouse down the street. Despite the language barrier, he was able to rent a room using the French francs the Maquis had included in his knapsack. Before even going upstairs to the room, he wolfed down several helpings of hot rice and beans. That was the first real food he had eaten since the stew he had enjoyed the last night with Robert and the other Resistance fighters. Then, once he was in his room, he soaked in a hot bathtub for over an hour. He fell asleep several times. Then he proceeded to sleep without dreaming for more than forty-eight hours. He would not remember waking up even once.

It took someone banging hard and relentlessly on his door to ultimately bring him back to life. He assumed it was the police.

Only later would he learn that they knew where he was all along and, despite their displeasure with his damage to their cell bars, had decided to leave him alone. They had notified the proper authorities, though. The knocks on his door were those of a representative of the US consulate in Spain. The man was there to see that Yeager went to better accommodations and to begin preparing him for his eventual departure from Spain.

When would that be? That was Yeager's first question. The man admitted he had no idea.

The date of his crossing into Spain was March 30, 1944. Three months before the launch of Operation Overlord, better known as D-Day, the Allied invasion of occupied France. That massive assault would delay Chuck Yeager's evacuation from Spain, but in an odd way it would actually aid his return to aerial combat in the skies over Europe.

He knew nothing of this, though, as he accompanied the consul representative to a larger city and much more impressive lodgings. In addition to Yeager, there were five other escapees there at the new spot, a resort hotel in the hot-springs spa city of Alhama de Aragón. Each of them was given money and was allowed to wander around the town, sightseeing, flirting with the women, and enjoying the healing springs, food, and drink. They were also given cigarettes by the consulate. Yeager did not smoke. Instead, he sold his smokes on the black market and made a tidy sum of money.

There was one major restriction during their stay. They were to be very careful about whom they talked with. They were to say nothing in public about who they were, where they had been before being shot down, their rescue by the Maquis, or anything related to the war and their part in it. They were not to venture too far from the hotel. For the diplomats to do their job, it would be necessary for Yeager and the other men to keep a low profile.

While it was not unpleasant duty at all, Yeager quickly became restless, ready to move on. The consul assured him that wheels were turning, negotiations were underway, but there was little sign of it day-to-day. The long wait began with Yeager having to cool his heels until another pilot from his squadron could come down from Leiston and personally identify him as being who he claimed he was.

Once Yeager's identity was confirmed, it opened the way for the Army Air Forces to notify his family that he was no longer missing in action. That he was not KIA, either. That he was very much alive, although there was little likelihood they would share with them his physical condition or exactly where he was. Yeager could only imagine how happily they would receive such good news. He figured his family would inform Glennis, too. Hopefully, she had not thought him dead and had by now been taken by some other hot-shot airplane pilot.

A major source of Yeager's frustration came from knowing that his squadron and many other pilots were flying off from their bases every morning, going out on missions, escorting the big bombers, engaging in frenzied dogfights, strafing Messerschmitts and Focke-Wulfs on the ground, and helping to win the war. But there he sat, basking in the sun at a resort hotel, soaking in the healing spring water of the area spas and eating very, very well. He would later claim he gained twenty pounds while being detained in Spain. And once he did make it back to his squadron, they gave him endless grief over the nice suntan he had gotten while all of them remained pasty white from being stuck in the cold mist at Leiston or shielded from sunlight by their flight suits, helmets, and goggles 30,000 feet above Europe. Most of them had what they termed a "raccoon look," tanned circles around their eyes where just a bit of sun could hit them around their goggles and helmet.

There actually were some complicated diplomatic negotiations going on at the time, the details of which Yeager and his fellow evaders were unaware. Spain was growing more and more desperate for petroleum. A deal was struck with Great Britain and the United States to trade fuel for Allied pilots. That would require a lot of petrol. Yeager would later hear that there were about 2,600 men who had made it across the border by that point. Now, in May of 1944, they were spread around Spain. They had arrived by various means, but many came by the same route as Yeager and Patterson, thanks to the French Resistance. Of course, there is no way to determine how many more died attempting to cross the Pyrenees. Or who gave up the trek and went back to take their chances in France.

Yeager would also never learn how many gallons of fuel he was worth in the transaction. Nor did he care. Not so long as it got him back to base and into a P-51.

It was mid-May 1944 when he and the others who were staying at the hotel were told to be prepared to catch a plane out of town on short notice. He had no idea where they were going when the plane turned south shortly after takeoff. Only when he saw the distinctive and famous 1,400-foot-high rock did he realize they were landing at Gibraltar. There they were turned over to the British and finally flown back to England.

However, Yeager would not be allowed to go back to his squadron. He was not issued a new flight suit or a new *Glamorous Glen*. His status remained murky. Nobody could or would tell him what was going to happen to him. All he knew was that he and the others who had come out of Spain on the flight back from Gibraltar were, at first, treated more like prisoners than thankful escapees.

Soon they were told that the Germans had been infiltrating with their own spies the downed pilots coming from France. Nazis who spoke perfect Americanized English and looked the part. They would take the identities of pilots who had been killed, hoping their subterfuge would not be discovered until they could ferret out and send back invaluable information.

But that meant any hope of getting back into the war had to be delayed another week or so until they could be interrogated by both British and US intelligence officers. It also meant still more frustration for Chuck Yeager.

There was no doubt in his mind that he would again fly over Europe on war missions. He had convinced himself that he could talk the Army Air Forces out of sending him back to the States. Yes, he knew the policy. Any pilot shot down and then evacuated—regardless of how great a pilot he was or how desperately the war effort needed him in an aircraft—risked compromising the Maquis and other French Resistance fighters should he again get shot down. The Germans had ways to get information out of anyone, no matter how resolutely the captured pilot might resist. And for that reason the Army's no-return-to-duty policy applied to Charles Yeager just as certainly as it did any other flyboy or soldier.

Still, he persisted. While waiting for new orders to be cut and even as transportation was being arranged for him to go back to the United States, Yeager began as vigorous a lobbying campaign as anyone had seen. He was demanding to become the first exception to the rule.

Even his buddies thought he was nuts. Why would anyone want to go back to such hellish combat? Even crazier, why would any pilot want to return to cold, damp, lonely Leiston, England? Not when he could freely and without shame go home to his family, his friends, and his beautiful fiancée. But Yeager explained to them that there were good reasons he wanted to go back and fight. First, of course, was the fact that he was convinced he was the best pilot there was, despite his so far unimpressive record. Only one kill before that German got lucky and jumped him. He knew he could make a difference against the Luftwaffe while redeeming himself.

Then there was the matter of his rank. He was proud that he was an officer in the Army Air Forces even though he had never spent one day in a college classroom nor attended West Point or any officer candidate school. If he went home now, he would never rise above the rank of flight officer. But if he got back in the air and showed what he could do, there was no limit to how far up the ladder he could move. He had already decided to make the Amy Air Forces his career if he were given the opportunity. However, if he was still a flight officer, he would almost certainly be cut loose once the war was over and there was no longer a need for so many pilots with such a low rank.

His buddies understood and urged him on, but all that logic fell on deaf ears in the command structure. There would be no exception. But as he did in most endeavors, Yeager persevered.

Clarence E. "Bud" Anderson was one of his Chuck's best friends in the squadron, his roommate once he got back to Leister, and someone who had gone most of the way through pilot training with Yeager. Anderson would conclude the war with seventeen kills, making him one of the top aces in the war in Europe and the leader among all the pilots in the 357th Fighter Squadron. He knew a good pilot when he saw one, even though Yeager had done little in combat action so far to prove it. He not only knew the West Virginian was a great pilot and would be an asset to the squadron should he be allowed to go back to fight with them; he also knew him well enough to believe that if anyone could talk his way back into a P-51 cockpit, it would be Chuck Yeager.

"If you were a military pilot, that was why you were there. To fight and fly," Anderson later wrote. "I doubt any other evader could have avoided being sent home. But Chuck was the most stubborn bastard in the world."

Anderson would later in life maintain that even though Yeager would gain fame for breaking the sound barrier in the Bell X-1, he was convinced that was not the epitome of his friend's aviation career. Anderson was convinced Yeager's experiences, triumphs, and stellar combat record in World War II were always of greater personal satisfaction to him, even if he did not talk about it as much as his other, more famous accomplishments.

"If he had done nothing more than [what he did in World War II] as a man and military pilot, he would have been satisfied with that," Anderson maintained.

But in late May of 1944, everyone was turning down Yeager's request. Paperwork was submitted to award him the Bronze Star for the unbelievable effort he made to save the life of Pat Patterson. (He did receive the medal with the V device, indicating the award was earned for valor in combat. The medal, V device, and ribbon are all currently being held by the Smithsonian's National Air and Space Museum in Washington, DC. Yeager and his wife donated the items to the museum.) He was repeatedly interviewed by both British and US intelligence officers about the specifics of his ordeal. He offered quite a bit of detail that could be of value to future soldiers and pilots who might be in a similar situation in occupied France. However, nobody seemed interested in his requests to go back to war.

Then Yeager received orders and a plane reservation. He was to leave England, bound for New York City, on June 25, 1944.

Eventually, Yeager had made his pleas to officers so far up the chain of command that, of necessity, he had to go to London to find those of higher rank. There he would talk his way into an appointment and speak with the higher-ups at Supreme Headquarters Allied Expeditionary Force in London. That would be the last resort. Truth was, no one could help him. But they were so impressed by this young flight officer with the easy drawl and steel-gray eyes, a fighter jockey who was flatly refusing to go home, that they humored him and agreed to hear his arguments.

That was when Yeager's efforts ultimately paid off. Much had changed in the time that he was being shuttled around from Bordeaux to the South of France, slogging over the Pyrenees and into Spain, cooling his heels in Alhama de Aragón while diplomats swapped gasoline for pilots, and then waiting for the orders that would send him back home. By now the Allies had gone ashore at Normandy and were advancing across France. The Maquis had come out of the shadows and had become an open fighting force, supporting the Allies. There was no real purpose any longer in protecting their identities and methods. The change from underground to foreground by the Resistance was front-page news in the Paris papers.

Yeager was passed even further upstairs and was finally able to make his plea before a two-star general. As others further down the chain had been, this major general was impressed with Yeager's story as well as his intense desire to continue fighting. The general told him, though, that as far as he knew, the only one who could make such a decision would be General Dwight Eisenhower. He just happened to be the supreme commander of the Allied Expeditionary Force in Europe, the top man running the war in Europe. A man who had just overseen D-Day and was very much tied up with its aftermath and progress. Although he saw no chance that Ike would honor Yeager's request, the major general did think the supreme commander would appreciate meeting a young man so determined to go back and fight for his country when he did not have to. He made Yeager an appointment to meet personally with Eisenhower the next morning.

That meant another night in a hotel in London. A night in which Yeager experienced what he initially decided was a bad omen. As he stood at the window in his hotel room, watching the skyline of the city, a German V-1 flying bomb suddenly roared low overhead and crashed only a block or two away. Yeager dived for the floor. He was not hurt. But when his racing heart slowed, he decided the close call was not an omen at all. It only served to anger him, and that steeled his resolve to get back into this war and put an end to what Hitler and the Germans were doing.

As the major general believed, the man who was running the entire war in this part of the world was very much impressed with Yeager, as well as another pilot, a bomber captain named Fred Glover, who was making a similar request for a waiver. The truth was, Eisenhower was just curious about two men who refused to go home and wanted to meet these crazy pilots in person.

"Look, boys," Eisenhower told Yeager and Glover. "I got guys out here shooting themselves in the foot so they can get sent home. You two have a free pass back to the States and you're bucking me on it. I don't understand."

Yeager tried to explain that he was a fighter pilot and a fighter pilot most wanted to fight. That was what he had trained for and that was what he should be doing.

Eisenhower could only shake his head. But he also admitted to the men that it was not actually his decision. It was a War Department rule that been handed down. Not even the Allied supreme commander could ignore the dictate. So he would have to ask for permission from someone else to send them back to combat. He promised he would do so.

Yeager was not optimistic. If the legendary Ike Eisenhower could not undo such a regulation, surely no desk jockey back in Washington could. It was a certainty as well that the general was pretty busy these days. He would not have time to argue the case for a couple of grounded crop dusters.

Yeager did not rest while he waited for the inevitable rejection. He talked his squadron commander into allowing him to fly over England as a way to maintain his skills in the Mustang, practicing dogfighting and strafing targets on the ground. He could also do good by showing newcomers how it was supposed to be done. His boss agreed to Yeager's request, but he was to remain under the strictest of orders to avoid any actual combat.

One day, while on a practice run with a group of newly arrived pilots, he and his wing mates received a radio call from the squadron operations officer.

"What's your location?" the operations officer asked.

"Twenty-five thousand feet over the base," Yeager responded.

"How much fuel you have?"

Yeager checked the gauge. In training so near the base, they did not carry the drop-away wing fuel tanks. He only had the tank in the fuselage behind his seat. But since they had not been playing with each other for long yet, he did have fuel remaining.

"About three and a half hours' worth," he said.

Then came the telltale question.

"You have live ammo loaded?"

"Yes, we do."

With that, they were ordered to go out over the North Sea and provide air cover for a dinghy filled with ten B-17 crew members who were in the water. They had crashed their heavily damaged bomber into the sea and were now out there in the little boat, bouncing around in rough water while awaiting rescue. The location was near the small archipelago of Heligoland, German territory, but in chilly waters not far from Denmark. If there was no cover protecting the downed men and the rescue boats on the way to pick them up, the Germans might decide to fly out there—with little risk—to where they were. The men in the life raft in the water would make easy targets. The British air-sea rescue boats would need to get there safely and then get them away from the cold water quickly, too. That meant not coming under fire from the Luftwaffe while they attempted the rescue.

It was a routine task for Yeager and his trainees, located not that far from the base. Maybe an hour of flight time out and another hour back. And in reality there would be little chance of the Luftwaffe sending planes out over the North Sea if they saw Allied fighters circling the B-17 survivors. A very small possibility of engagement. That was likely why Yeager and his students were allowed to do the job.

Yeager acknowledged the order and turned his Mustang to the northeast. No problem. He was just happy to be looking at some different territory.

But soon after locating the downed flyers and commencing to circle them, Yeager spotted something the other pilots around him were not yet able to discern—and likely would not for several more minutes. It was a German Junkers Ju 88, a twin-engine multipurpose warplane typically equipped with very dangerous and effective weapons. It was coming their way but had apparently not yet seen the Mustangs.

Yeager could only assume the plane was coming out from Heligoland to strafe the men in the sea. Although he was not supposed to be involved in any combat operations—by direct order—and certainly not over German territory, he turned his Mustang eastward and flew off to meet the newcomer and create some bluster. The least he could do was try to frighten the Ju 88 away from the guys in the drink below.

Sure enough, the Luftwaffe pilot wanted no part of the P-51. Upon seeing Yeager coming his way, he immediately turned 180 degrees and headed back toward Heligoland as quickly as he could. As Yeager continued pursuing—maybe farther than he realized—the enemy antiaircraft guns on the island began hurling flak skyward, trying to chase the American fighter off the tail of their Ju 88.

That angered Yeager. He chased on, closing to about two hundred yards, and opened up on the bigger plane. Direct hits! The Junkers virtually flew apart in midair. Then, with the remaining parts of the enemy plane trailing fire, smoke, and debris all the way, he watched with glee as it crashed in flames on the beach far below.

As Yeager turned back toward England, he was already wondering how he would explain this to his squadron operations officer. He had disobeyed a direct order. That was something he never did, no matter how silly it might be. But he had gotten carried away with all that pent-up fighting fury inside him.

The bomber survivors down there in that life raft deserved his best shot, too.

All the way back home, he continued to hope that he could avoid getting chewed out for doing something he had been directly ordered not to do: engage the enemy. But he had shot down a German plane. That should count for something.

He was unable to avoid the wrath of his boss, though. He got a big-time tongue-lashing.

"Dammit, Yeager, can't you do anything right?" his commander fussed. "We'll all be court-martialed!"

Yeager did not try to deny what he had done. The camera on his plane had captured the entire incident. The footage would have made a great training film for new pilots to learn how to pursue and eliminate an enemy warplane. But it also was proof that Yeager had blatantly disobeyed orders. The squadron officer, to save his own skin, came up with creative ways to get around Yeager's transgressions.

First, the film of the shoot-down was given to another pilot. He was told to claim it as his own handiwork. The encounter report would be submitted under his name as well. Not Yeager's. That would give the other pilot full credit for the elimination of the Ju 88. The operations officer did not realize at the time that when this bogus kill was claimed and credited, then combined with the pilot's previous claims, the lucky guy would then have a total of five. That made him an "ace," compliments of Chuck Yeager.

There was more. Yet another pilot in the squadron would get credit on his record for the combat time that had, in reality, been flown by Yeager. That effectively swept the whole thing under the rug.

Chuck Yeager? He got credit for nothing. But he was now officially grounded. And the next airplane he was supposed to climb into would be the passenger plane bound for New York City, ending his combat career before it ever really got started. He would be credited with only one kill, the one on his seventh patrol, the day before he was shot down.

In a sad footnote, the pilot who earned ace status by Yeager's having taken down the Ju 88 would never claim a legitimate fifth kill. On his next mission, he was shot down over France. He survived the incident and soon joined and fought with the French Resistance. However, shortly after the D-Day invasion, he was killed in combat.

The very next day after the Ju 88 incident, Yeager was presented with a summons back to the squadron operations officer's headquarters. He fully expected his boss was calling him back to tell him that his orders had been changed, accelerated, that he had a minute and a half to pack, and then he was headed back stateside. Or worse: he was going to tell Yeager that he was about to be court-martialed.

Yeager was correct about one thing. His travel orders had been changed. But not accelerated. They had been canceled entirely. That desk jockey at the War Department in Washington, DC, had ultimately decreed that the supreme commander, Eisenhower, could make the ultimate decision on whether or not to allow Yeager and the other crew member, Fred Glover, to stay and fight.

And General Eisenhower had promptly given them the thumbs-up. Years later Yeager would again visit with Eisenhower. Ike was by then an ex-president of the United States, but he remembered well the details of meeting with Yeager and his fellow pilot that day in London. He maintained that he had actually followed Yeager's career and, when he realized Yeager was deeply involved in the Vietnam War, he summoned him to a meeting. He wanted to learn more about what was going on in Vietnam, where Yeager was then flying combat missions from the Philippines.

At any rate, Chuck Yeager was back in the war. Now all he had to do was go over there to the other side of the channel and North Sea and make all this hiding, sneaking, waiting, begging, and politicking worthwhile.

"For me," he later wrote, "the real war had now begun."

THIRTEEN

GLAMOROUS GLEN II . . . AND III

Within two weeks, my tan was gone, and I had lost the
twenty pounds I gained in Spain. I was back to being skin
and bones with two sunburnt circles around my eyes, a
Leiston raccoon.

    —Chuck Yeager, describing his return to aerial combat
    after his ordeal in France

M uch had changed from March 5 to mid-May 1944, from the time Chuck Yeager made his way back from getting shot down near Bordeaux to the time he rejoined his squadron in Leiston. He expected the reunion to be brief. He had been notified that he would be sent back to the United States toward the end of June. He found it to be a sad occasion when he did get to see his squadron mates—not just because, as far as he knew, he would never fly another mission with his buddies but also because of the attrition among his fellow fighter pilots.

When he finally got Ike's okay to resume his job, he found that only about a dozen of his old pals were still flying for the 357th Fighter Squadron. Some had been killed. In all, about 26,000 members of the Eighth Air Force died in World War II.

The fates of most of the men who, like Yeager, had been shot down and were yet unknown. Still others had been transferred out to other units or, their duty done, sent home. These were men who had been through so much together, some good, some bad. It was a strong brotherhood, a bond that was difficult to break.

Yeager was happy to see that good friend Bud Anderson was still there, though. Anderson's roommate had just been transferred, so he invited Yeager to move in with him. Normally, combat pilots avoided forming close friendships. There was too great a likelihood that one would be killed. So, to avoid that kind of hurt, such attachments were typically shunned. Not Anderson and Yeager. Although it had only been about a year since they had first met, and both men were only in their early twenties, the two pilots considered themselves old friends. That was likely in part because they had so much in common. But it could also be attributed to the fact that they immodestly considered themselves to be the two best fighter pilots in the Army Air Forces. And each slightly favored himself over the other.

Anderson had already accumulated a combat record that strongly backed his contention. Yeager was hoping to soon prove his own bold claim.

Anderson would later write that though neither he nor Yeager loved war, they loved flying and especially dogfighting. They did not particularly enjoy killing Luftwaffe pilots, either, but they both considered that their most intense thrills came when they were successful in shooting airplanes out from under the skillful, well-trained Germans. Now, since permission had finally been granted for Yeager to return to combat duty, the two were convinced they would have plenty of opportunities to participate in that kind of air combat action.

Yeager would always attribute to Bud Anderson the coining of the phrase that referred to air combat as the "college of life and death." He was referring to the fact that pilots matured very fast in war. Otherwise, they did not survive it.

There was another major change about to come that would take some getting used to for Yeager. But it was a positive one. War leads to innovation. The Army Air Forces continued to improve the P-51 Mustang fighter aircraft, even though it was already one of the war's most effective planes. The Germans certainly were not standing still in their development programs. Neither were the Japanese. The Allies had to continue to push forward, constantly creating, building, and testing equipment to keep them a step ahead of the enemy if this war was to end as an Allied victory.

Chuck Yeager's first plane upon his return to air-to-air combat—*Glamorous Glen II*—was a P-51C, a P-51B variant. Although the specifications were almost identical to the P-51B from which he had been forced to parachute out of over France, it did have some noticeable differences. It had a Merlin engine, but this one had been developed and built by Packard, not Rolls-Royce, and they were constructed in Dallas, Texas, rather than in the Los Angeles area. They still came from the factory with a couple of issues, changes that generally got addressed as effectively as possible once they were delivered to wherever they were to be used. Those included having poor visibility to the rear because of the construction of the cockpit canopy and a tendency for the gun behind the propeller to jam while the pilot was doing maneuvers that drew excessive g-forces. Only about 1,700 of the C-variant Mustangs were ultimately delivered. However, most of those would still be in use at the end of the war. Despite their limitations, the P-51C was a very effective airplane for the job they were doing over Europe.

However, Chuck Yeager would not be in a 51C for long. He flew the C-version *Glamorous Glen II* for only a few months. Then he was issued a P-51D. His new plane did not come to him directly off the assembly line in Dallas. No, his next airplane was already being flown by another pilot in Yeager's unit, Captain Charles K. Peters, a man who was to be sent home as soon as he returned from one last mission over enemy territory. On that particular run, Yeager made certain to take extra care to protect the short-time pilot. Peters flew as Yeager's wingman on his final mission and there were constant reminders over the radio and by hand signals that the pilot was to be very cautious with Yeager's next ride.

Yeager already knew that if Peters made it back to Leiston, that P-51D would have *Glamorous Glen III* painted on its nose—covering up the airplane's previous name, *Daddy Rabbit*—before the next morning's briefing was finished and he rode out to the flight line to take her to war.

The mission started smoothly enough. Then, sure enough, in keeping with Yeager's recent run of sorry luck and close calls, as the bombers they were escorting dropped the last of their loads and made the big turn back toward the English Channel, *Daddy Rabbit* suddenly developed one huge problem, abruptly dropping out of formation, the Mustang's nose headed almost straight downward, toward German soil. That unexpected move came just as Peters and all the other fighters had jettisoned their auxiliary fuel tanks, ready to dogfight if there should be any challengers chasing after them.

"Damn engine just quit," Peters radioed.

Although he had no idea what he could do to help, Yeager dropped away from the other planes and followed *Daddy Rabbit* down. By the time he lined up on the stricken plane's wing, they were passing through 5,000 feet of altitude, less than a mile from the ground, and still falling fast. Even worse, they had by now plummeted to an altitude at which they found themselves amid all the thick flak the German guns were hurling skyward, even though the bombers and the rest of their escorts remained high above it all.

That was when Peters reported that he was about to bail out. That he would allow Yeager to climb back up to relative safety, above all that hot metal that was exploding around them.

"No, you don't!" Yeager told him. "We'll figure this out and you won't put a dent in my airplane."

With that, Yeager tried to keep the other pilot calm while he directed him in taking a good look at every gauge on his panel. But also, as the flak grew even more dense, tracers from machine guns on the ground were already reaching to a point just below them, and the heavily forested ground was becoming more and more defined. And deadly real.

Then Yeager had a sudden thought. Something that had happened to him a time or two while flying over a desert somewhere in the western United States as he learned how to keep these birds in the sky.

"Check your fuel mixture," he suggested. It was most likely the final idea he could come up with. His buddy would have to bail out in mere seconds. And Yeager's prospective new ride would be a smoking hulk down there among the trees with no effort from the Nazis at all.

Suddenly the plummeting Mustang's engine came to life with a beautiful puff of blue smoke. The propeller began to rotate. Peters pulled back hard on the stick and then, once again under power, began a steep ascent out of all the mess popping around them. Yeager followed as closely as he dared.

"Must've hit the fuel mixture control when I pulled the wing tank release," Peters admitted on the radio, sheepishness obvious in his voice. "Went to emergency rich and she fired right up."

"Good job."

"Thanks, boss."

Although he absolutely wanted to, Yeager said no more. At least not until they were safely back above Great Britain, lining up for landing at Leiston.

"Dammit, *Daddy Rabbit*. You land that thing, park it, and give me the keys!"

Peters only acknowledged with a couple of bumps of the push-to-talk switch on his microphone. There had been far too many of their wing mates lost on what was to be their final mission before going home. The curse of the short-timer. This one had been too close.

The P-51D was a noticeable upgrade to both the 51B and 51C, even faster and more maneuverable than its predecessors, and it came with six .50-caliber machine guns instead of the standard four. Most of the Mustangs were already being supplied with .50-caliber armor-piercing incendiary ammunition. Those did considerably more internal damage to enemy aircraft than the traditional ammo. The first of the newest planes had shown up in England just in time to contribute to the D-Day landings, where they did a fine job of providing cover for the invasion forces.

Besides its upgraded firepower, the most obvious development on the P-51D was its bubble canopy, which offered the pilot an unobstructed 360-degree view from the cockpit. It had been made possible by the creation of a type of plexiglass that allowed the canopy to have large curves but still remain free of visual distortion. The pilots loved it. It did not completely negate the Luftwaffe's favorite tactic, slipping up on Allied fighters from behind, but the full-circle sight line made that trick far less effective for the Germans.

Later in 1944 a new gunsight was being installed on the Mustangs as well. It actually included an analog computer into which the pilot entered the wingspan of the target and the range. The so-called lead computing gunsight handled all the calculations for aiming the plane's guns not to where the enemy plane was but to where it would be when the bullets arrived at that point in the sky. Then all the pilot needed to do was fire when ready.

The P-51D eventually became the most prolific Mustang

model manufactured. More than 8,000 units would be delivered by the end of World War II. German fighter pilot Kurt Bühligen, the third-highest-scoring Luftwaffe pilot on the Western Front, was quoted as saying of the P-51D, "It was perhaps the most difficult of all Allied aircraft to meet in combat. It was fast, maneuverable, hard to see, and difficult to identify because it resembled the Messerschmitt Me 109."

For the rest of his life, anytime Yeager spoke of the Mustang, he credited that airplane for changing the course of the air war in Europe. "It made the difference," he would boldly state. But he also typically cited the skill and bravery of P-51's pilots, too.

Even so, Chuck Yeager would likely have flown a crop duster off to combat by the time he was finally allowed to take off on his long-delayed ninth mission. He was raring to go. Then reality set in. While he had been hiding in barns and toolsheds and hiking across the Pyrenees, the air war over Europe had cooled considerably. At least for fighters escorting bombers.

The Germans simply did not have enough fighter planes and pilots to attempt to challenge the bombers and their deadly escorts with the force they once had. Antiaircraft guns were not able to send flak high enough to deter the B-24s and other heavy bombers that were doing horrible damage to cities in Germany, including Berlin itself.

The liberation of Paris in late August of 1944 was another major event that signaled a waning war. That final battle came when the French Resistance staged an uprising against the German garrison in the city even as General George S. Patton and his Third Army were approaching. Together, they made quick work of retaking the "City of Lights."

Yeager and his fellow fighter pilots sat around inside a hut they had proclaimed to be the "officers' club" at Leiston, lamenting the lull in the skies. Happy as they were to see that the Luftwaffe had apparently given up, they still longed for the kind of action they had experienced over the last three-quarters of a year that many of them had been there.

That certainly included Flight Officer Chuck Yeager. He had come to the war with high hopes and great expectations. And that was not just his own outlook. Most of the others in his squadron considered him to be the consummate fighter pilot. He possessed not only the remarkable eyesight but also the natural instincts and extension-of-the-aircraft physical attributes, too. But there was also his intense desire to shoot down every enemy aircraft that carried the swastika insignia. In any dogfight, he aimed to be the most dogged fighter pilot.

But his time at the controls of a Mustang had so far been, by his own estimation and when measured against his hopes, a colossal bust. He had arrived in England just before Christmas of 1943. He flew his first combat mission in February of 1944. He had done his job protecting B-17s and B-24s and other members of his fighter squadron, and he had strafed plenty of ground targets, but it was not until March 4 that he had claimed a Messerschmitt Me 109 as his first kill. And as it turned out, his only kill for months to come. That was because he got himself shot down the very next day.

Although he was fortunate to survive that ordeal, and

appreciated the risks taken by the French, and especially the Maquis to get him to Spain and back to England, he had still proven nothing. Not to himself. Not to his squadron mates. And certainly not to the Army Air Forces brass. Now he was eager to fly, and there were a lot less targets up there for him to spar with.

Yeager remained supremely confident in his abilities. Most everyone who knew him was, too. But he still had nothing to show to back it up.

Of course, the war was not yet over. There was still danger aplenty. Now that the Germans no longer seemed capable of mounting any kind of significant air challenge to the bombers, the American fighter pilots were given new goals and tactics. Now, after they had escorted the bombers over their targets and then safely back home over no-longer-unoccupied territory, the fighters often turned back, dropped down to lower altitudes, and attacked anything that moved in Germany or other occupied areas. That included convoys, trains, airports, river traffic, trucks loaded with troops or military equipment on roadways, and more.

This was dangerous work for sure. There was often no way to know if there were gun emplacements near whatever it was that the squadron was pummeling. Then a sudden shot, or an unnoticed German fighter plane coming in out of the sun, could take out one or more of Yeager's team.

The men who had been around the longest, the original group who had sailed to the war aboard the *Queen Elizabeth*, grew into an even more unified brotherhood. They all moved into the same living quarters at Leiston. They spent almost all their time together, usually in the "officers' club." The tall tales grew even taller and more far-fetched. They took runs together on the train to London when they had a few days off duty. They conducted their own rudimentary version of dogfighting, but it took place not among the clouds but in a field near their quarters. And they were riding bicycles instead of zooming about in their P-51s. They also used their Army-issue .45 pistols to shoot at the plentiful rats that inhabited the base. Sometimes they hit their targets. More often they merely punched holes in the corrugated iron walls of the Nissen huts. All this activity helped. It allowed them to blow off a bit of steam between missions.

Yeager would later tell of going off into the nearby woods and hunting local game, dragging back and dressing his bounty, then cooking it and feeding it to his buddies. Sometimes, those hunting trips took him to private hunting preserves. There were also rumors of him making "emergency landings" in open fields in France, returning to base with fresh vegetables and fruits. Once he landed at Leiston with a full case of wine bottles on his lap to celebrate some event or another.

As Yeager waited for more air-to-air combat opportunities, he embarked on another quest. He still held the rank of flight officer, roughly equal to the Army's warrant officer designation. He firmly believed he had earned a promotion to lieutenant, a commissioned-officer rank. There was a practical reason for the promotion, too: because of his obvious abilities, he was now most often designated as squad leader on their missions. That meant he was boss, regardless of his or anyone else's rank. There was no question about Yeager's flying prowess or his ability to lead a squad. However, some captains and even lieutenants took issue with obeying commands from someone they did not consider their equal—in rank, that is. This attitude had the potential for making already dangerous situations even more lethal. Up there, one person had to be in charge.

Those who flew with Yeager had no doubt that he deserved a higher rank. He was a born leader and seemed to have a second sense about where to fly and how to place his team to be most effective, even in the most complicated or chaotic action. Despite having a reputation as a hard charger, someone willing to take risks in order to claim enemy planes or ground installations, the truth was that he was not at all prone to do anything ill-advised or foolhardy. Most of his fellow pilots trusted his judgment and could cite instances in which he had avoided combat or flew right on past potential targets simply because he deemed it too precarious to attack.

Yeager knew he had two strikes against him when it came to receiving a promotion. The most obvious was his lack of a college degree. There was nothing he could do about that except continue to fly circles around those who had completed West Point or graduated from some other college or university.

However, the other big negative was even more difficult to overcome. That was the court-martial for accidentally shooting the farmer's horse while on guard duty at Victorville, California, back in '42. No matter how well he flew his plane, he could not remove that ugly blotch from his service record.

Then, after having been denied promotion three times, the board of colonels ultimately relented on his fourth try. He became a second lieutenant. That still left him ordering around most of the others in his squadron who outranked him. But at least he was now a commissioned officer. And that removed a mighty burr from beneath the saddle of Charles Elwood Yeager.

It did not necessarily solve the problem of some of the higher-ranking members of his squadron choosing to ignore a shavetail lieutenant. Even while they were flying a mission and he was designated as commander of the unit.

So, as Yeager typically did, he cut to the chase when such a thing happened. On one mission, when a captain refused to obey Yeager's order to close up and fly in tight formation, the newly minted lieutenant pulled out of the pack himself to straighten the guy out. He slipped around behind the uncooperative pilot without being noticed. Then he fired a few rounds just above the slacker's canopy. Once the reluctant pilot realized it was his designated unit leader and not the Germans that were shooting at him, he quickly did as he had been told.

Later, when the captain filed a complaint against Yeager, the two of them were called before the squadron commander. After hearing both sides of the story, the captain was promptly transferred out of the squadron and Lieutenant Yeager was praised for his leadership, unorthodox as it may have been. Everyone knew that not obeying the orders of the unit leader could be dangerous for everyone. Even deadly. It was not a time to question anyone's educational achievements or command pedigree.

It was about this time, in late summer of 1944, that Chuck Yeager took notice of the fact that there were now more than twenty "aces" in the 357th Fighter Group. Officially, to be designated as an ace fighter pilot, he would have to get credit for causing the crash of five enemy planes. So far, the self-designated "best fighter pilot in the Army Air Forces" had a grand total of one kill.

One. And with fewer and fewer opportunities to tally any more. There was no ace credit for "shooting down" a barge on a river or leaving behind trucks in a convoy smoking and in flames. Yes, that kind of action helped win the war, and that was the real goal. But it certainly would be good if he could only get those other four German pilots to auger in so he, too, could claim the status he knew he deserved. In his heart Chuck Yeager was already an ace. He only needed the tally to prove it to everyone else.

The concept of becoming an "ace," as well as the term itself, came out of World War I, the first conflict in which airpower played a major role. And especially air-to-air combat, or dog-fighting. It actually emerged as a form of propaganda. All participants in that brutal war needed heroes, and a pilot who excelled in taking down enemy airplanes in such dramatic fighting was a natural for the media. French newspapers were the first to establish the designation—*l'as*—for one of their pilots who had been credited with shooting down five German aircraft. That number stuck.

When World War II ended, and all the data had been tabulated, the top American ace was determined to be Richard Bong, who took down forty enemy planes in the Pacific theater. Gabby Gabreski of the US Army Air Forces was the American ace in Europe with twenty-eight kills. Germany would have several pilots who claimed more than a hundred takedowns. Such high counts were primarily because those men flew far more sorties than did the Allies, the Luftwaffe necessarily kept their pilots in service longer, and they had no restrictions on how many times a man could be shot down, rescued, and returned to service to fight some more. Certainly nothing like what Chuck Yeager had experienced. Much of their air combat came over German-occupied territory, too. Luftwaffe pilots had to be either killed or captured by the Allies for their flying days to come to an end. German records indicated some of their pilots had flown more than a thousand missions, but many had bailed out at least twenty times. Little wonder they each could have more aces and more kills than the Allies.

Still, Yeager had not given up on the possibility he could still earn that status. He certainly was flying plenty of missions, but the job and the enemy response had changed dramatically.

Then, in mid-September 1944, Yeager would finally get that second "kill." Never mind it was only half credit, one that he had to divide up with another pilot who decided to help make sure the German was finished and followed him down to fire off a few bursts of his own. The British—who used the showbiz term "star turns" instead of "kills"—had adopted the policy of having pilots share credit when both men had contributed in any way to the enemy aircraft's destruction. The US Army Air Forces followed suit.

It was September 13, 1944, and Yeager was leading the "Blue Flight" as escort for more bombers, intent on pounding Hitler and the Nazis until they would finally give up this madness. As the B-24s dropped their ordnance and made the turn back toward home, Yeager spotted a single Messerschmitt Me 109 far below, diving at about 15,000 feet. Although the German seemed to have no interest in coming after the bombers, Yeager, without hesitation, made his own quick nosedive, chasing after the enemy craft.

By the time he caught up with the Messerschmitt, both were angling downward at almost 500 miles per hour. Yeager could feel the heavy hand of gravity on his chest. But he had the guy dead to rights.

As he would later write in his encounter report, "I closed up fast and started firing at 300 yards. I observed strikes on engine and fuselage. The engine started smoking and windmilling."

The Messerschmitt was going down. No doubt about it. But another pilot, Lieutenant Frank Gailer, zoomed in from above as Yeager flew right on past the target and had to do a big roll to come back around to try to make sure he had finished the guy off. However, Gailer fired several bursts from his .50-caliber machine guns as the German attempted to crash-land his airplane on its belly in a field. That was all it took. The Me 109 augured in with a big, fiery explosion.

Yeager did come around in time to take a picture of the crash. He then flew past and saluted Gailer as they climbed back to join the squad and continue on toward home.

Yeager would note in his report that the new computerized K-14 gunsight that he used in the attack was "very satisfactory."

He also held no ill feelings about Gailer taking part in the attack. The German pilot might have been able to land and walk away from the plane had his squad mate not finished him off. The 109 could have possibly been recovered, repaired, and put back into service. Had that been the case, neither American could have counted this as a kill.

"I claim one Me. 109 destroyed (shared with 2nd Lt. Frank L. Gailer)," he wrote in the encounter report.

At least it got him a half step closer to becoming an ace. And that dogfight for partial credit was about to finally open the floodgates and allow Chuck Yeager to prove to the world that he was the natural-born fighter pilot so many were convinced he was.

FOURTEEN

FIVE MESSERSCHMITTS OVER BREMEN

"Flier Bags 5 Nazi Planes to Vindicate Ike's Ruling"
—Headline in *Stars and Stripes* newspaper,
October 18, 1944

He could not believe the carnage he was seeing 5,000 feet below where he and the rest of the two squads he was leading were now flying lazy circles. In a joint mission with the RAF, American C-47 Skytrains had dropped paratroopers into enemy-occupied territory near the seacoast in Holland. Once on the ground and after securing the immediate area, they had begun setting up bridges and establishing operations in preparation for a larger invasion to follow. That part of the operation, mostly on the first day, had gone relatively well.

On the second day, the Skytrains were to tow in and release gliders filled with troops, jeeps, artillery, and medical units. It was that part of the operation that Yeager and his fellow fighter pilots now looked helplessly down upon. The transports and gliders alike were taking a brutal pounding from Germans on the ground, from machine guns, mortars, and artillery. As he watched, Yeager saw several of the bigger planes take direct hits and go down. And they could see gliders literally coming apart when they hit the ground after having their wings shot off or getting blown in half by the ferocious barrage. Few were reaching their designated landing zones. Several did not even make it to shore and went down in the water.

Yeager was leading the fighter squads under orders to supply air support for the Skytrains but to stay out of the landing zone. They were there in case the Germans sent planes to intercept the RAF planes. As much as he wanted to, he could not dive and strafe those gun emplacements that were wreaking havoc on the aircraft below. Picking off the gliders like they were little more than clay pigeons. The fighter planes were under strict orders to remain above 5,000 feet. But at this rate there would be few C-47s remaining for them to support. The frustration level was intense.

It was September 18, 1944, only five days after Yeager's half-credit kill over Kassel, Germany. And his frustration level was once again mounting.

The one thing that gave him hope was that he was by then almost always being chosen as group commander, leading several squads on missions. He figured that if he was so often on the point, he would be more likely to be the first to spot approaching German fighters. The first to break formation and go engage.

But the lull continued. It was a good thing that bombers could now complete their mission without running into so many enemy fighters intent on blowing them out of the sky, as had been the case only a few months before. The action that Yeager and the other fighters saw was still against ground targets, and they took full advantage of that. But he still needed three and a half more kills, and it was beginning to bother him. Still, he sucked it up and did his job. As he would later tell an interviewer, "The enemy is a guy you have to kill." It did not matter if that was in a tense dogfight or strafing a troop train.

Then, on October 12, he finally got his chance. And he made the most of it.

Yeager was leading three squadrons that were escorting a box of B-24s on a daytime run well into Germany. He decided to order two of the squadrons to continue to fly in formation with the bombers while he took his own guys, Cement Squadron, and raced out to run nearly a hundred miles ahead, trying to pick up any Luftwaffe fighters that might be trolling about for Allied bombers.

They saw nothing. Just a nice day with a brilliant sun highlighting the colorful changing leaves on the trees in the forestland far below. They were between Bremen and Hanover, approaching the deep-blue waters of Lake Steinhude, when Yeager spotted a swarm of "gnats" crossing their path from about 1100 to 0100 and at about the same altitude as he and his wing mates, 28,000 feet.

Yeager did not bother to radio the other pilots flying behind him. They would see what he saw soon enough. There certainly were enough of them. And soon Cement Squadron was within a mile and a half of a whole flock of German Me 109 fighters. Yeager took a quick count. Twenty-two of them. And they obviously had not spotted the American planes yet, since Yeager's guys were coming at the enemy from out of the dazzling afternoon sun.

Being the leader in the formation had paid off. Yeager pulled ahead of the others and settled in behind the enemy fighters as if he were once again flying tail-end Charlie, but this time for Hitler. He took his Mustang up to 30,000 feet and remained in formation for a full three minutes, slowly creeping up to within 1,000 feet of the last of the Messerschmitts. Then he would be within point-blank firing range.

The leader of the enemy squadron apparently had not yet seen Yeager and his guys approaching from out of the sun. Or if he had, he must have assumed these were only more Me 109s come to join the ambush party for all those B-24s approaching from the west.

But then two of the Germans near the back of the formation did notice the P-51 flying brazenly along, infiltrating their neat bunch. Those two had apparently been lagging, running outside the otherwise orderly formation. And when they spotted Yeager, they clearly panicked.

Panicked and banked—one left and one right—directly into each other, slamming together hard.

Yeager snorted. What was all that noise about the wonderfully skilled Luftwaffe fighter pilots? He would later learn that the Germans had declared that they would rather replace airplanes than have to replace pilots. In most cases, they were under orders to bail out of a damaged plane even if they thought they could save it instead of trying to nurse it to a safe landing. That was exactly what those two pilots did.

As Yeager eased in and lined up his sights on one of the birds, both canopies suddenly opened and flew off the planes.

Then their pilots fell away from their plunging fighters, deserting their planes in midair.

Damn! Yeager thought. Two kills and he had not yet fired a shot! Who knew it could be this easy?

But there were twenty more Jerrys dead ahead. As he ordered the rest of the squadron to come around and join him in the fun, he jettisoned his wing fuel tanks to gain speed and maneuverability. Now he was ready for the one thing he felt he was born to do. He was about to throw the next punch in one hell of a dogfight.

Yeager grinned when he noticed that all the planes he could see—American and Nazi—were simultaneously dropping their fuel tanks. It almost looked like a bombing run. That also meant the Germans now knew they were about to be in the middle of some serious air-to-air combat. But Yeager, for the moment, was the only Mustang within firing range. He had been on the radio and the others would show up shortly. But for just this moment all those 109s were his for the taking.

Their tail-end Charlie was suddenly within 600 feet. Using his new high-tech gunsight, Yeager cut loose.

"I observed strikes all over the ship, particularly heavy in the cockpit," he would later write in his encounter report. "He skidded to his left and was smoking and leaking coolant and went into a slow diving turn to his left."

Yeager thought for a moment about following the wounded plane down, to make sure he was done for. But there were far too many healthy targets directly ahead of him. He flew back up a thousand feet higher and picked out his next victim. Another pilot from the American squadron, just arriving on the scene, would later report that he saw that Me 109 fully ablaze, spinning out of control as it plunged past him.

Three kills! In less than a minute. But he had no time to consider that he only needed a half credit to become an ace.

The next target in his sights had taken a dive to the right. Before Yeager could slow, he was beneath the German plane and at a range of a hundred yards. But he was ready to shoot. He would have to unleash a burst at 10 degrees off angle if he wanted to hit the guy without having to zoom past and pull back around for a better shot. The German or one of his squad mates would likely be shooting at him from a superior angle by the time he could complete that maneuver, though.

"I gave about a three second burst and the whole fuselage split open and blew up after we passed," he would report. Scratch one more Messerschmitt.

Four! But he still had no time to ponder his having just reached his goal of becoming an ace fighter pilot. There were more targets buzzing all around him, and he was already presenting a lovely target as well for all those Germans zooming around the October sky like a swarm of angry hornets.

Almost immediately after watching kill number four come apart in the sky, he saw another Me 109 directly to his right, obviously off the throttle, slowing, doing all he could to get behind Yeager's P-51. He could not allow the guy to gain that superior position. He slammed his plane into a hard skid, drawing almost paralyzing gravity force in the process that shoved him hard into his cockpit seat. It was all he could do to keep his hand on the stick and move his head to see where he was going. He would later credit the relatively new gravity suit the pilots were now wearing for keeping him from passing out cold during the maneuver. More than a few fighter pilots had blacked out during close combat, and that almost always proved fatal. That lifesaving suit was also a benefit with which the Germans were not blessed for much of the war.

But Yeager's wild move worked. In completing the impossibly sharp turn, he passed almost within touching distance of the German plane's tail. Somehow, Yeager managed to complete the high-g maneuver, with *Glamorous Glen III* creaking and groaning with the strain but remaining intact. He got back around and lined up as quickly as he could behind the enemy plane. He could only imagine how impressed the German pilot likely was with the impossible move Yeager had just made. Then, although he was still "skidding"—basically flying sideways—he was able to fire a short burst from three hundred yards. He saw potentially fatal hits on the wings and tail section of the Me 109.

"He snapped to the right three times and then bailed out when he quit snapping at about 18,000 feet," Yeager wrote.

Five kills! Not only had Yeager hit his goal, but he had become a rarity for American pilots. He was an "ace in a day." And since he witnessed the pilot bailing out this time, it was an easy kill to verity. If the pilot left the plane, there was nobody else aboard to fly it. And even a fine warplane like the Me 109 could not land itself.

In addition to the G suit, he would once again credit in his report the new K-14 computer gunsight for helping him stalk and shoot down his fifth aircraft that day.

After noting in the encounter report that the Luftwaffe had

modified the color scheme of their Messerschmitt fighters—they were now "a mousey brown color all over" and with "a purple nose"—Yeager flatly stated his assertion for this mission: "I claim Five Me. 109s destroyed," he wrote, and noted he expended "587 rounds .50 cal MG" in accomplishing the feat.

Once back to Leiston, Yeager caught grief from the pilots and leaders of the other two squadrons who had been left behind, still escorting the bombers. They had listened in to all the action on their radios. That provided them a good play-by-play account of what was obviously an action-packed fight. But when they attempted to get Yeager to give them the coordinates where all the fun was, and to give permission for them to join in, he had ignored their transmissions.

"There weren't enough Krauts to go around," he later explained in his long, slow drawl and with a broad grin. The fact was, of course, that by the time they got there, most of the action would have been over. And it was not an option to leave the bombers unprotected. There easily could have been another German squadron out there, lying in wait for them.

He also caught grief for having two of his kills occur without him even heating up the barrel of his .50-caliber.

He maintained that just the sight of *Glamorous Glen III* was all it took to send the guys out of their cockpits, their warplanes abandoned midair.

The next week's edition of *Stars and Stripes* made much of the angle that Yeager was only in the cockpit of his plane and in position to become an ace in a day because of General Eisenhower's okay for him to return to combat.

"A ruling by Gen. Eisenhower last July cancelling the orders which would have returned 1/Lt. Charles E. Yeager, Mustang pilot from Hamlin, W. Va., to the US after being shot down and wounded in enemy territory and getting back to England proved to be bad news for the Luftwaffe," the article reported. "The 21-year-old squadron leader, who holds the distinction of having led his group while still holding the rank of flight officer, last Thursday bagged five Messerschmitt 109s over Bremen. 'I had to go through a lot of channels to see Gen. Ike,' he related. 'I went from one office to another and from one high officer to another, until I found myself in front of his desk.'"

Yeager would be awarded the Silver Star with bronze oak leaf cluster—the third-highest award for valor in combat—for taking down the five enemy fighter planes that day. As they did with his Bronze Star, Yeager and his wife years later would donate this award to the National Air and Space Museum at the Smithsonian Institution.

After having a chance to think about the incident, Yeager decided and would henceforth say that he believed the swarm of German planes that day were in the process of forming up, getting ready to take on the American bombers. When Yeager and his squadron came zooming in from out of the sun, the Messerschmitt pilots mistook them for another Luftwaffe squad joining the attack. That was why they allowed the Mustangs to get among them. By the time they realized who had joined the scrimmage—and a couple of Messerschmitts took each other out with no shots fired—it was too late. Game on.

So now that he had achieved one of his most coveted goals, what would Lieutenant Yeager shoot for next? Simple. Do it again. He knew there were numerous German pilots who had made ace in a day multiple times. Some as many as five times.

If it helped win the war, Yeager figured it was worth trying. But in the meantime he was about to go out there and shoot down something totally different. Something most folks had never seen before, including ace pilot Chuck Yeager.

Something new and revolutionary.

FIFTEEN

SCRATCH ONE SWALLOW

*I split S-ed on it and was going around 500 M.P.H. at 500
feet. Flak started coming up very thick and accurate.*
　　—Chuck Yeager's encounter report description of
　　　his attack on a German jet fighter plane

A lthough he was keeping a busy schedule—much of it assigned by the US Army Air Forces but plenty of other
activities that were decidedly not official business—
Chuck Yeager still managed to write at least two letters a week
to Glennis Dickhouse back in California. And others to his
folks in West Virginia every week or so, too. He could not tell
them much at all about the war and what he was doing out
there over France, Germany, and other hot spots in central Europe. Not even about his remarkable accomplishment, becoming only the third US pilot at that point in the war to become
an "ace in a day."

He did share plenty with them about poaching pheasants
and other game birds on nearby estates and cooking them up
for the rest the squadron. He also told them carefully selected
details—his mother would not have approved of some of their
activities—of all the shenanigans and tricks they continually

played on each other, even when they involved considerable imbibing of spirits, sometimes cheap beer, but other times the best Scotch whisky or French wine they managed to acquire in truly creative ways. There was plenty of mischief that occurred on trips to London, right there in Leiston, in various places on the European continent (sometimes involving expending leftover ordnance at unsuspecting targets), and in many spots in between.

All that horseplay was simply a way to handle the intense pressure these men dealt with most days. The knowledge that they would be attempting to cheat death every time they answered the early call, ate a hasty breakfast as they absorbed the mission briefing, strapped themselves into the cockpits of P-51s, and rumbled off the runway and into the thick overcast over the English Channel and North Sea. It should be noted, too, that even calling them "men" was a stretch. Most of the squadron members were in their early to mid-twenties. Chuck Yeager was still twenty-one years old in late 1944.

There was one other unclassified thing Yeager never mentioned in his letters to Glennis. That was marriage. He claimed he felt he never had to say anything. Just by the way they talked in their correspondence was enough to verify that both of them knew it was a done deal. Besides that, he admitted he was superstitious. Had he specifically mentioned getting hitched, he would have almost certainly put a hex on himself. Then he would have augered in on one of those few remaining missions and there would have been no wedding. That was "Fatalist Chuck" again.

He did write of his impending marriage to Glennis in his letters to his family, though, just as certainly as if he had already gotten down on one knee and proposed. It was a foregone conclusion as far as he was concerned. He and his best friend, Bud Anderson, were already planning to have a double ceremony since Anderson had a similar understanding with his own fiancée. Now they only needed the Army Air Forces to cooperate and send them back to duty at the same base stateside. Or at least give them enough leave to take care of such matters if they had other plans for the two ace pilots.

There was always the chance, however, that the Army Air Forces would have no need at all for Yeager once the war was over. Never mind that he had earned the status of ace. That he was most often a squadron leader, chosen ahead of others with higher rank and a college degree. And despite the fact that he had earned a promotion to the rank of captain in the fall of 1944. Yeager had never gotten over his inferiority complex, although he had proven himself not only equal to but in most respects better than everyone else with supposedly superior qualifications. In light of that possibility, he had told Glennis that the only thing he could promise her was a "cabin in a holler" somewhere in West Virginia.

Yeager was perceptive enough to know that there were too many captains who wanted to be majors, majors wanting to move up to colonel, and all of them angling to become generals. A career high-ranking officer's life was considered relatively easy duty for twenty years or so. Then came retirement while still in his forties and a chance to double-dip, collecting retirement pay while beginning a new career.

However, that was not what motivated Chuck Yeager to want to become a career Army Air Forces officer. He just wanted to fly airplanes. All kinds. Teach others the correct way to fly them, too. And help develop new tactics and hardware that would keep America militarily superior as a deterrent to future wars. Especially superior in the skies and beyond. Note that becoming a test pilot was still not one of his aspirations. He assumed that he would never qualify for such a highly technical job.

It was November and the weather had turned especially cold and damp. It had become difficult for some of the pilots to remain motivated. The remaining few members of Yeager's original squadron had now been stationed on the eastern shore of Great Britain for almost a year. Unlike many of their group, they had somehow survived scores of dicey, dangerous missions. But they kept reminding each other that although the war had turned, that the Allies' march across Europe was making progress toward Hitler's backyard, that even though it might soon finally be over, it was still dangerous out there. Their jobs remained critically important.

The Germans had certainly not surrendered or given up any ground easily. Like a wounded animal, Adolf Hitler had become even more dangerous and determined to do whatever it took to save the Third Reich. V-2 flying bombs continued to hurtle into London and other English cities. The brutal Battle of the Bulge was about to begin in mid-December of 1944 as a last-gasp effort by the Germans to split the Allied invasion troops and recapture Belgium. The aim was to try to rekindle their chances of making a comeback, of still winning the war. The Luftwaffe was even putting into service some innovative new weapons, long in development, but so far slowed by the war itself. One of those new weapons was the Messerschmitt Me 262 jet-powered fighter aircraft.

The Me 262 would become the world's first operational jet-powered warbird. The fighter version was dubbed the "Schwalbe" ("Swallow") and a model specially modified to be used as a small bomber was called the "Storm Bird." Recognizing the value of speed in an air war, the Germans had begun development of the jet before the war even started. Due to many problems—some of them political, with infighting among Hitler's high command over the ultimate value of such a craft— the first planes did not fly with jet engines until July of 1942 and only became fully operational in the summer of 1944. Even so, it remained a very limited part of the Luftwaffe arsenal.

The plane was effective primarily because of its speed. It was easily capable of flying at greater than 515 miles per hour at level flight, more than 90 miles per hour faster than the P-51D Mustang as typically equipped. The Germans were able to use the 262s to fly in, attack Allied bombers, and then zoom away from the P-51 escorts, knowing they could escape without risk of a skirmish with the fearsome Mustangs. The Swallows were not necessarily built for dogfighting, sacrificing maneuverability for raw velocity. That was a valuable and lethal commodity, both in arriving without detection and departing with no fear of being chased down by any plane in the Allied fleet.

The Allies met the challenge of the jet fighters by launching attacks on fuel storage facilities that held the particular petroleum recipe required by the jet engines. They also concentrated on factories in which they knew the aircraft were being constructed. It was eventually obvious that there was no way the

Germans could continue to import the specific metals and parts necessary for the construction and maintenance of the Swallows. The Luftwaffe instead resumed their emphasis on aircraft types that could more easily be manufactured and put into the air at such a desperate time for the Nazi war effort. That renewed concentration came at the expense of the jet fighters.

The otherwise revolutionary aircraft had one other major vulnerability and the Allies would soon begin taking advantage of it. Chuck Yeager just happened to be one of the first to do so.

As difficult as it was to chase and intercept one of the Me 262s, the plane was an easy target during the few moments when it was taking off or attempting to land. Its engines did not provide nearly enough thrust when flying at low airspeeds. The response of its throttle was notoriously slow. That meant pilots had to be especially cautious during takeoff and landing. If Allied fighters were only able to zoom in on the jets during those maneuvers, they had a good chance of taking them down. But that also meant having to fly low over airfields that were heavily protected by antiaircraft guns.

Still, despite facing ferocious "ack-ack," the primary susceptibility of the Me 262 was what allowed Chuck Yeager to be among the first pilots to shoot down one of the German jets.

On November 6, 1944, he was leading the White Flight of Cement Squadron at about 8,000 feet over the coal-mining town of Essen in western Germany. There were plenty of clouds about that day, so they were almost on top of a formation of three Me 262s racing past at about 3,000 feet below them before anyone—even Chuck Yeager—spotted them. Their path would take them directly below his squadron. So far the Germans had not shown any indication that they had seen the four Mustangs above them, either.

Yeager knew what they were and how fast they could be gone. He immediately broke formation and dove at the three Swallows, fully aware they might pull up and engage. But, more likely, they would simply kick their throttles and disappear into the dense clouds and mist. Before they could do either, he settled in on the last Swallow in the loose V formation and, when he was within four hundred yards, let loose a burst from his guns. Maybe, coming in unseen from the higher altitude and out of what little sun there was, he could land a knockout punch on at least one of them. His flight camera would later confirm that he had several hits on the German plane that was his primary target and a few more on another one he had not even been aiming for.

The jet pilots still seemed to take little notice of Yeager, his Mustang, or the other planes in White Flight. Nor did getting bullets through their wings seem to bother them all that much. They took no evasive action or made any move to challenge anyone in air-to-air combat. Instead, they simply ramped up their jet engines, raced away, and were quickly gobbled up by the low stratus clouds.

"They . . . seemed to depend on their superior speed," Yeager wrote in his encounter report. "They pulled out of range in the haze."

Yeager could only shake his head and marvel at a bird that could fly so fast. What must it be like to have that much speed at your bidding? He later wrote, "I was a fat man running uphill to catch a trolley." Though he was flying at near 450 miles per hour, the Messerschmitts had left him behind as if he were standing still. Yeager was jealous. And frustrated.

He eased back up to 8,000 feet to look for the other three P-51s in his flight but saw nobody. Not unusual. The potential targets had left the scene so quickly, the other American pilots likely never had a chance to even consider joining any ambush. The clouds had grown thicker, too. Yeager assumed his wing mates had headed on toward home and he would catch up with them before they reached the coast and the North Sea. Then he would give them a bit of flak for not trying to help him chase down those jets.

Along the way, he was flying through a cloud deck when he noticed the overcast appeared to end abruptly off to his right. He decided to ease over that way, hoping he might once again spot the formation of Swallows. He also dropped down below 5,000 feet, where the air was even clearer. Sure enough, he saw three Me 262s—maybe the same ones—now flying much slower and at an altitude of about 2,000 feet, their direction of flight exactly opposite to his. His first thought was that they must be preparing to land. Yeager was very much aware that if this was the case, it would be the perfect time to attack them. Sluggish as they were while approaching an airfield, they would not be able to run off and leave him this time. At least not all three of them.

And then he could see a sizable airfield in the distance below. His guess had been correct. They were landing. And this absolutely was the opportunity for which he had been hoping.

He instinctively began a split-S maneuver. That was something a fighter pilot typically did to quickly disengage from midair combat against an enemy aircraft. A way to rapidly go in the opposite direction and get away from something or somebody. Not this time. The split-S was the fastest way for Yeager to give chase on three highly desirable targets.

Without even thinking about it, he knew the best way to surprise these speed demons was to get behind them as rapidly as he could. He would fly into a position so he could come at them from their blind side and just above them as they slowed even more to set down on the runway.

He put *Glamorous Glen* into a quick half-roll, which left him flying upside down. Then he brought her around in a big half-S-shaped arc so he could get behind the Swallows, flying right side up once more. It was what many would consider a daring maneuver. Yeager only thought of it as a necessary one.

When he was upright again and flying level, he was only five hundred feet from solid rock and dirt. But he was once more fully focused on locating the three jets. However, now he saw only one of them. The other two had apparently pulled away to go around and allow the leader to set down first. And that one was going at best estimate only about 200 miles per hour—200 miles per hour and still slowing noticeably.

That Swallow was now a sitting duck.

As he homed in on the 262, Yeager hardly noticed the first smudges of flak flaring up in the mist and scarring the sky ahead of him. When he was within four hundred yards of his target and had set the target site, he let loose with a burst of gunfire and immediately saw significant hits on the jet's wings.

Meantime, the flak had grown much thicker and better aimed, exploding all around his plane. He could hear some of the stuff rattling off his fuselage. One solid hit and he could well be out of commission. One strike on the Mustang's cooling system and he would be immediately without power to climb. He was going over 400 miles per hour and only about five hundred feet off the ground. If he did get hit, he likely would not have time to jettison the canopy and bail out. Even if he could, he probably could not get the parachute open in time to lessen his impact with the ground.

Again he relied on instinct. There was only one best way to escape this wall of antiaircraft fire. He pulled back hard on the stick and climbed about as straight up as the airplane would go without stalling and falling back to earth. As he did, he twisted in his cockpit seat to look down, back behind him, trying to determine if he had done enough damage to the Swallow to claim it as a kill.

Sure enough, he would report, "I saw the Jet E/A crash land about 400 yards short of the [air]field in a wooded field. A wing flew off outside the right Jet unit. The plane did not burn."

There was smoke and dust everywhere, though. That Swallow would fly no more. And he was soon high enough above the ground that the antiaircraft fire was no longer a threat to *Glamorous Glen.*

Yeager made a few more circles around the airfield, hoping to see the other two jets attempting to land. Nothing. Nor did he see any traditional fighter planes coming up to try to chase him away. Flak or not, he would have dived on the other two if he had had the chance. But still no sign of either jet. He reluctantly turned westward, into the sinking sun.

It was only then that he finally had a chance to consider just how thick that flak had been down there as he pursued the jet fighter almost down to the tarmac. He would later admit that his hands were shaking on the stick and his heart was pounding fiercely as he banked hard and flew on toward England.

Once again he had cheated death.

"I claim One Me. 262 Destroyed and Two Me. 262s Damaged," he submitted on his report. The two damaged were those he struck with bullets during the initial encounter. All three claims were confirmed by the camera mounted on his airplane.

Yeager would later write, "I'd rather have brought down the son of a bitch in a dogfight, but it wasn't exactly an easy kill, one quick, accurate burst, with flak banging all around me."

He was among the first but would not be the only one to take advantage of the Swallow's weaknesses. Although jet-powered aircraft would become the norm in aerial combat over the next few decades, and especially during the Korean War and in Vietnam, the Me 262 would not have any serious impact on the outcome of World War II. Perhaps if it had been adopted earlier and, like most wartime technology, honed and improved along the way, it could have been a much bigger factor. It could be argued, though, that Chuck Yeager's willingness to dive into a sky full of deadly flak on November 6, 1944, and take down that one unfortunate Swallow ultimately helped assure the limited effectiveness the jet fighter would have in this particular war.

Others would recognize the reality. Just the possibility of having aircraft that could fly at a velocity approaching the speed of sound—and maybe past its invisible barrier, should it be confirmed that such a feat was even possible—also encouraged other nations to continue designing, experimenting, testing, and innovating, often using the Me 262 as a model to emulate. That would be the future.

There is also considerable irony in having a pilot whose name would one day become synonymous with aircraft speed—only three years in the future—being one of the first to shoot down a jet plane.

(There is still some speculation about who was the very first pilot to shoot down a jet warplane. Some maintain it was Chuck Yeager on November 6, 1944. Other Allied pilots had forced Me 262s into the ground in August and October, but none of them had fired a shot. Five Royal Canadian Air Force pilots claimed to have jumped a Swallow on October 5, fired on it, and done some damage that may or may not have forced it to go down. They did fire, they did hit the jet, and it did crash, so many consider that as being the first jet warplane to be shot down. For his part, Yeager never specifically made such a claim. He did like to say in interviews, "The first time I saw a jet plane, I shot it down.")

For his bravery and skill that November day, Chuck Yeager was awarded the Distinguished Flying Cross. That medal was given to any person serving in any branch of the military who "distinguished himself by heroism or extraordinary achievement while participating in an aerial flight. The performance of the act of heroism must be evidenced by voluntary action above and beyond the call of duty." The very first DFC had been awarded to Captain Charles A. Lindbergh for his historic solo transatlantic flight in 1927. And as with his other medals, Yeager's Distinguished Flying Cross was donated to the Smithsonian's National Air and Space Museum.

The day after claiming the Swallow, Chuck Yeager was back in the air, flying even more low-altitude missions, strafing and bombing ground targets, once more daring antiaircraft gunners and the occasional fighter plane to shoot him down. "It was a different war at fifty feet," he later said. And the shorter his time grew until his deployment to Great Britain was up, the more the old superstitions about short-timers and bad luck preyed on his mind.

As it turned out, he had at least one more spectacular feat to accomplish in the war, and it would come three days before Thanksgiving, on November 27, 1944. He would describe it as a "dream day" for a fighter pilot. That wild action would result in Yeager officially becoming a "double ace," and it would be a battle that many consider the biggest Allied air victory of World War II, although one in which the newly minted captain would witness something so awful that it would often crop up in his nightmares for the rest of his life.

But at least he would live to talk about the whole episode, the good and the horrible, for many years to come. And that worry about being a short-timer would prove to all be for naught.

SIXTEEN

A FIGHTER PILOT'S DREAM

The squadron turned left and we saw two gangs of E/A.
One was 50 plus; the other was approximately 150 plus.
Cement [squadron] leader told me to take over.

    —Lieutenant Charles Yeager, combat report for action
    on November 27, 1944

In many ways, it was like the early days of his duty in the war. Chuck Yeager was again flying top cover for a daylight bombing mission. This time, though, there were no B-17s or B-24s. Instead, it was a group of P-51D Mustangs that were carrying bombs designed to penetrate earth and blow up underground fuel storage tanks. Each plane carried one bomb, but it was heavy enough to limit the smaller plane's maneuverability.

The target this day was way beyond Berlin and eastern Germany, in the city of Poznan, Poland. Yeager led White Flight, a covey of four Mustangs. His best friend, Bud Anderson, was in command of the entire Cement Squadron.

It was a spectacularly clear day, unusual in these parts for the end of November, but a decidedly nice sky for flying. It would have been easy to forget that the world was still at war.

That those planes a few thousand feet below Yeager's underbelly carried bombs destined to wreak havoc on one of Poland's oldest and most beautiful cities, formerly a center of culture and the arts. But now many of the townspeople had either been expelled, murdered, or forced into performing labor for the Nazis. Its 2,000 Jewish citizens had already died, mostly in nearby concentration camps. More than 95,000 Germans had been moved to the area, primarily to help prepare the city as a key line of defense against Russian troops, now advancing westward. Poznan would fall to those Russian invaders in February of 1945, leaving in ruins what few of its monuments and striking architecture had not already been destroyed. That included a statue of former US president Woodrow Wilson, honoring him for his efforts to help Poland in the aftermath of World War I. (It would be replaced with a new statue in 1994.)

November 27, 1944, had already been a deadly day. A German V-2 rocket exploded in the streets of Antwerp, Belgium, just as an Allied convoy was passing through. More than 150 people died, including 29 American soldiers.

There was soon be another vivid reminder that the war was still underway, even on a rare sunny day. And as was typical, Chuck Yeager and Bud Anderson were the first in Cement Squadron to see it coming.

Later it would be determined that German radar had painted an incorrect picture of the herd of bomb-bearing Mustangs and their P-51 escorts. They were flying in a reasonably tight formation and the Luftwaffe believed them to be a group of B-17 Flying Fortresses or B-24 Liberators. Furthermore, what they believed to be bold American heavy bombers appeared on their radar screens to be flying unescorted. This offered a rare opportunity. Fighters from airfields all over East Germany and Poland were ordered to get airborne and attack as quickly as possible.

The resulting battle would be one of the biggest air-to-air combat showdowns of the European war. On a perfect day for a man convinced he was put on this earth to dogfight in an airplane, Chuck Yeager would find himself in the middle of the action. He later remarked that skirmishing in a cloudless sky full of enemy aircraft with a fine airplane beneath him, plenty of ammunition, and adequate fuel in his fuselage tank was "a fighter pilot's dream."

At about 1:00 p.m., shortly after spotting what appeared to be an odd dark cloud in an otherwise clear sky, Anderson reported there were at least 150 enemy fighters at Cement Squadron's eleven o'clock. Yeager already had his extraordinary eyes focused on another group approaching from a different angle. There were at least fifty planes in that flock. Cement Squadron consisted of sixteen P-51Ds. Even so, Yeager liked their odds.

Rather than be frightened or unwilling to engage, Yeager would later recall, "We couldn't believe our luck. We plowed right into the rear of this enormous gaggle of German fighters."

He had long since decided that the skills of the current crop of Luftwaffe fighter pilots were poor. Intelligence reports confirmed that, due to lack of fuel, training had been greatly curtailed. The number of planes capable of flying had dwindled, mostly due to problems with replacement maintenance parts but also to lack of factories to build replacement aircraft. And to put into the air the limited number of aircraft the Germans did have, they had begun placing instructors in the cockpits instead of having them training a new crop of pilots.

Still, here they were, over enemy territory, and there were more than two hundred enemy fighters coming their way. Coming quickly. Once the Germans realized they were encountering a flight of Mustangs rather than bombers, they would still be intent on stopping Cement Squadron from accomplishing whatever they were bound to do.

"You're closer and in the lead, Chuck," Bud Anderson radioed. "You take over."

"Roger."

Yeager quickly turned so he would pass ahead of and at a higher altitude than the smaller group of attackers, likely before they had spotted the Americans, and then he could climb even higher above and behind the larger bunch. From there, he could take his pick of targets. Lord knew, there were plenty from which to pick!

The rest of his own flight followed him closely, and only a bit farther back, as did the rest of the squadron. Shortly, though, each pilot would be on his own, concentrating on his own targets.

As he always tried to do, Yeager put *Glamorous Glen* into a position between one of the enemy stragglers and the early-afternoon sun. From that position, he not only had the element of surprise but also a good look at the whole tableau. And quite a scene it was!

Hundreds of enemy fighters. Some of his own group, already diving on and shooting at German planes. Despite expecting to find unescorted heavy bombers, not a couple of score of

Mustangs, the Luftwaffe pilots had quickly realized that they would have to fight their way out now, and they were doing just that. Thankfully, Yeager could also see that another group of Mustangs was arriving on the scene, just in time to join the melee.

But now he had a bead on one of the stragglers, a Focke-Wulf Fw 190. A big grin spread across his face. He had a perfect setup on the son of a bitch. The pilot had not even bothered yet to jettison his wing tanks, so he would be sluggish.

And it seemed like poetic justice that it was an Fw 190. Just like the one that had shot him out of the sky over Bordeaux, made him walk across the mountains in the snow, and had kept him out of the war all that time when he could have been making a difference. Little chance it was the same guy. Even so, revenge at 32,000 feet was about to be very, very sweet.

"I jumped the last E/A, which was a Fw 190," he would write in his encounter report. "He went into a rolling dive to the right and then pulled up into a tight turn to the right. I shot a side deflection shot from the right and got hits from around 200 yards."

A side deflection shot meant he was firing at a point where he anticipated the target to be when his bullets got there, or: "Don't shoot where they are. Shoot where they're going to be." More good advice from Grandpa Yeager, but he had been talking about crows and rabbits, not German fighter planes.

Yeager followed the target as the pilot tried to continue his escape turn, even though the enemy plane had suffered severe damage. He watched as the aircraft's tail simply fell off in midair. The 190 went into a wild, end-over-end plummet, with fire and smoke everywhere. Too much torsion for the pilot to even get his canopy open and bail out before his fighter disintegrated underneath him.

"I saw no chute," Yeager would report, and his camera would confirm it.

He did not linger. There were almost two hundred other potential targets waiting for him. He pulled up sharply and began searching. Everything was above him then. That put him at what he considered to be a severe disadvantage.

Sure enough, literally from out of the blue, another Fw 190 jumped him as he was climbing back to where the action was taking place. It was mostly due to luck and the Luftwaffe pilot's poor aim that the sneaky German's first barrage missed *Glamorous Glen*. That gave Yeager the opportunity to turn right into the mugger and get off a deflection shot at a mere one hundred yards. He was close enough to see the other fighter pilot's eyes but not well enough to verify if they were wide with fear. But they should have been. Yeager had the angle on him already and he would shortly become another dead duck.

"I got many strikes on the fuselage and the E/A started smoking and went into a dive," Yeager later recounted. "I followed it down to about 15,000 ft. and the E/A flew apart. There were no chutes."

He had clicked the button to start his camera. The US Army Air Forces could admire his handiwork later. And verify his second kill of the day.

Chuck Yeager was being completely accurate when he later wrote "no chutes" in the encounter report. However, as he followed his second kill of the day downward to make certain the battered aircraft was done for, he witnessed a sight that would haunt him the rest of his days. Just before the plane came apart, the pilot jumped from the cockpit.

As Yeager watched, the man's unopened parachute pack was ripped away from him by the air from the plunging fighter. The man tumbled and fell toward the ground with nothing to slow his descent.

Yeager had heard of it happening to American pilots, but he had never seen it before. They sometimes neglected to tighten and fasten their parachute harness, whether for comfort or simple forgetfulness. Most times they did not even realize what they had done until they landed safely and began to unbuckle to exit the cockpit.

This German 190 pilot had recognized his mistake much too late.

Fifty years later, Yeager would write in his autobiography, "To this day, I can still see him falling."

But now there was more work to do. Yeager was well on his way to becoming a double ace, a total of ten enemy planes shot down, putting him in a truly rarefied atmosphere. Hell, with all those targets up there, he might make "ace in a day" again, too. He pulled hard on the stick and zoomed back up toward 30,000 feet, already angling for his next victim from the buffet of choices available to him. He caught glimpses of fellow squadron mates and they were mostly all engaged in dogfights. Others were trying to be. It was a sight he had never encountered before on this scale. It was exhilarating!

Airplanes zoomed all about, shooting at each other. There was an uncountable number of ugly smudges of black smoke all about, like potholes in the bright, clear sky. Then, when he glanced down, there were parachutes—pilots from both sides—while the farmland five miles below was littered with smoking, burning airplanes. Focke-Wulfs. Messerschmitts. Mustangs.

"I climbed back up to the tail end of the gang and jumped another straggler."

These Luftwaffe guys were definitely not as good as the first ones he had encountered almost a year before. They seemed lost. Confused. Or scared. They had no idea how to try to evade a West Virginia squirrel hunter who might be angling to draw a bead on them. He was determined to make another one pay for the lack of preparedness and loyalty to that madman Führer of his.

"The E/A started a circling turn with me . . . I turned in and closed up to about 100 yds. and shot a 30 [degree] deflection and got hits all over the ship."

Kill number three! Again he tailed the smoking, disintegrating aircraft down to about 25,000 feet. This time the pilot made it out and his parachute immediately billowed up above him. This guy might even make it back to his *Fräulein*.

As soon as Yeager saw the chute open, he pulled hard on the stick and headed upward again, checking his fuel as he climbed. He had plenty. Lots of bullets left, too. Thank goodness for a fine aim and the computerized gunsights.

"I started back after the large bunch and saw another lone 190 circling around over to my left." Were they not teaching Luftwaffe fighter pilots to try to stick together during air-to-air combat? American pilots were constantly on the radio, warning their buddies about approaching enemy planes. That was because they were close enough to see the threat. This guy was either badly trained or just plain dumb. Either way, he was about to get what he deserved. "I got into a lufberry with him and again closed up within 100 yds. at around 40 [degrees] deflection at 29,000 ft."

The German pilot had resorted to a World War I air defensive maneuver called a lufberry, or more commonly "lufbery." Named for French ace Raoul Lufbery, the tactic required a plane under attack by an enemy aircraft to fly in a tight horizontal circle in the air. One problem for this pilot: for a lufberry to be effective, there must be other friends nearby. The idea was to expose the attacking fighter to fire from others in the group as he chased the target in circles. There were no more German fighters anywhere close enough to help.

"I fired a short burst and all the hits were concentrated in the cockpit," Yeager would report. "A sheet of flame came out of the cockpit and the E/A nosed down in a dive, on fire."

There would be no parachute this time, either. Yeager followed the blazing Focke-Wulf down to 12,000 feet. Kill number four, confirmed!

There were more, though. Once more he yanked back on the stick and headed as quickly as possible for where the larger group of Germans had been. But on the way the radio crackled with the words, "Bogie down south!"

It took Yeager a few seconds to realize that one of his own squadron was reporting him as an enemy fighter coming up from far below. Then it occurred to him that only one person could possibly spot him from that far away. That was Bud Anderson.

By then Yeager could see that the remaining enemy fighters were hightailing it home, diving for the deck. The fight was mostly over. But with adrenaline still flowing freely, he took his Mustang up to where Anderson was flying circles, looking for stragglers. Once he was sure there were none, Yeager "attacked" his buddy with all the ferocity of a real dogfight. The two of them whooped and hollered on their radios as they conducted as spirited a session of air-to-air combat any of the remaining members of Cement Squadron had ever seen.

Only then did they turn and head back over Germany toward England.

Yeager would have his four kills—and double-ace status—confirmed. Anderson had three kills that day. In all, the Germans lost almost a hundred fighters in the battle. Eleven Mustangs went down.

They inadvertently ventured off course and flew through heavy flak on the way home. But they made it back to Leiston and staged a big celebration that night. For Yeager's four kills. For his recent promotion to the rank of captain. For Anderson's promotion to major. To mark the first-year anniversary of their arrival in England.

It was a wild party and helped everyone avoid thinking about fellow pilots who had been lost in that day's amazing action. The next morning's hangover was not even enough to make any of the men regret the legendary gala. Now, though, there was much for Yeager and his contemporaries to consider.

Rumors were rampant that Hitler could not possibly keep the war going beyond spring. The Russians were advancing across eastern Europe and being very brutal about it. The other

Allies continued their march, coming from the west, too. There was other scuttlebutt, though, that Hitler and his top leaders would never surrender until the last SS soldier was dead. Others claimed the Führer was developing a megaweapon, one capable of killing millions, and would not hesitate to use it on Paris or London.

Everything Chuck Yeager was seeing had him convinced that the Nazis could not last much longer. The war could well be over before the summer of 1945. Regardless, it was likely about to be over for him anyway. At least the part in which he was an active fighter pilot dodging and darting over hostile territory.

He was among the last three men remaining from the original *Queen Elizabeth* group. He had only eight more missions assigned, all of them scheduled in the first half of January, starting on New Year's Day. If he survived all eight, he would turn twenty-two years old the day before Valentine's Day in February 1945. From what he could determine, he could well be in the United States by then to celebrate it. Maybe by getting married to Glennis, alongside Bud Anderson and his fiancée.

So all he had to do was continue pressing the war for a little bit longer but avoid getting himself shot out of the sky in the few weeks he had left.

★ SEVENTEEN ★

MASTERY OF THE AIR

They have complete mastery of the air. They bomb and strafe every movement, even single vehicles and individuals. The feeling of helplessness against enemy aircraft has a paralyzing effect, and during the bombing barrage the effect on inexperienced troops is literally soul-shattering.

—Field Marshal Erwin Rommel, commander of
the German 2nd Panzer Division, describing the
Allied air war in Europe

For the remainder of his days, in speeches, presentations, and interviews around the world, Chuck Yeager would often talk of the horrors of war. Not defensively or to minimize the cruelty of the things he was called upon to do in a quest to restore peace. He noted that those actions were directed against a vicious enemy that had launched a brutal war—an enemy that did not always follow the previously-agreed-upon civil conventions. He and his fellow fighters went out to achieve victory by whatever means necessary. He felt strongly that having the best equipment, the most well-trained and experienced fighters, and the will to go into battle and win it were the best way to avoid having to fight a war in the first place.

What he most enjoyed, felt the proudest of, and was most positive about was dogfighting, one man against another man, playing a game of skill and resilience like the knights of old. The better pilot usually won. Often, with two good pilots battling each other, they would both fly away, living to maybe challenge each other another day.

Anytime he talked or wrote about the war, he made it clear he did not necessarily enjoy taking the life of the other pilot. "You fought wide open, full-throttle. With experience, you knew before a kill when you were going to score. You set him up, and there was no way out. Both of you knew he was finished. You were a confident hunter. Your trigger finger never shook. When he blew up, it was a pleasing, beautiful sight. There was no joy in killing someone, but real satisfaction when you outflew a guy and destroyed his machine. The excitement of those dogfights never diminished. For me, combat will always remain the ultimate flying experience," he would write.

Of course, he only experienced about a year of it in World War II. And much of what he had to do during the war was, at least in his eyes, not nearly so elegant or knight-like. Or enjoyable.

The worst—and the missions he most dreaded—were the low-level bombing runs and strafing attacks. Not only were they dangerous but they were often made against what were only marginally valid military targets. He had no problem shooting at troop convoys, military staff cars, or freight trains obviously loaded with ammunition and supplies for the soldiers that were shooting and killing Allied troops. After all, when asked later about killing men, he was the one who said, "An enemy is just a guy you have to kill."

But there were times during his experience in Europe when he received an assignment he strongly considered ignoring.

In October of 1944, in an effort to further demoralize the German people and maybe even force them to revolt against Hitler and the Nazis, Yeager and his squadron mates were dispatched on a mission to a 250-square-mile area inside Germany. They were to dive on and shoot any target that moved, military or noncombatant. Distasteful as it would be to fire on civilians, Yeager would follow orders. He always did. Maybe he bent them a bit at times, but only when he thought the mission might be more successfully accomplished by doing so.

When talking about these kinds of missions, Yeager would always relate what he told one of his fellow pilots during the briefing for that particularly distasteful strafing run: "If we do stuff like this, we damn well better make sure we win the war."

Throughout the rest of his life, when talking about the horrors of war, he would always talk of his own internal arguments, considering both sides of the situation. A farmer digging potatoes might seem a terrible target for a pilot and a fine warplane like the P-51D. And a cruel thing to do. But that farmer was almost certainly feeding SS troops with his crop. SS troops who were killing American soldiers. Was it really much of a stretch to consider him to be a military target?

Of course, the Germans often fought dirty. Yeager recounted an incident in which several planes in his squadron were diving to strafe a train. But as they drew near, they saw it was clearly marked as a hospital train. They took their fingers off their triggers and began to pull up and seek another target. But suddenly the side of one of the train cars dropped away, revealing machine guns. They opened up on the American planes, taking one down and killing its pilot.

Yeager also had vivid memories of the atrocities committed by the SS against civilians while he was being hidden and moved about from town to town by the Maquis. He was also very aware of how he would have been treated had he been captured. The Geneva Conventions in effect at the time defined the basic rights of wartime prisoners, civilian and military, and provided protections for civilians in a war zone. Although Germany was a signatory to the agreement, German forces were often guilty of ignoring its tenets. That made it marginally easier for Yeager and his fellow pilots to follow orders that were often odious. Actions that would, nonetheless, nag him for the rest of his life.

At the time, though, he tried not to think about it. He was, no matter how hard he tried, becoming more and more superstitious, leery of what those final couple of weeks might bring in the way of short-timer bad luck. It was not only when flying missions, either. One night, just after lights out, they heard the rumbling of the engines of a big airplane of some kind. Not American or RAF. It was a Nazi bomber. The men all dived beneath their bunks in the barracks, fully expecting a bomb to drop among them. It never came. The plane did strafe the mess hall but it was empty at that hour, so nobody was hurt. Yeager chose to take it as a positive omen, just as the German rocket outside his hotel room had been the night before he met with General Eisenhower. That had turned out pretty well, after all.

Yeager would later talk about how the war for him and most of his fellow fighter pilots had become almost routine by late fall of 1944. "We probably were at our peak," he recalled in later years. "That was because we flew every day, six to seven hours, in the same airplane, and we shot down quite a few German airplanes. We were probably the most experienced fighter pilots that ever existed. We knew we could handle anything the Germans could throw at us. And we could handle any German pilot that came up in any kind of airplane. That was because we had demonstrated it, time after time. We really felt at home in the sky."

As his tour of duty drew shorter, he could take pride in what he and his buddies had accomplished over there. The Allies had, in fact, achieved air superiority over Hitler's domain. They were doing their part in the Battle of the Bulge, which many considered would be the final showdown of the war. Although bombing missions were still dangerous duty, pilots often returned to base reporting no enemy contacts.

The Mustangs of Jimmy Doolittle's Eighth Air Force had certainly done their part. Chuck Yeager and his mates would eventually be credited with shooting down almost 6,000 enemy aircraft.

A part of him wanted to stay longer, continue to press the enemy, and shorten this war. But another part of him was ready to move on to whatever was next for him. In the meantime he would do what he was told, fly those final eight missions, and then, when the Army Air Forces were done with him there, he would head for home.

But it was not going to be quite that routine. A few days before Christmas, he was summoned to the CO's office. Men from British intelligence were there to meet with him. They had a job for him. He was to fly *Glamorous Glen III* down to an airfield in Lyon, France, and from there he would be whisked away to a mysterious destination where he would take part in some kind of clandestine mission. Before he knew it, he was checked into a luxury hotel in Geneva, Switzerland, with absolutely no idea why he was there or what the Brits expected him to do.

He found out the first evening when he was invited to dinner with a gentleman named Peter DePaolo. Foreshadowing Chuck Yeager's future claim to fame, DePaolo was a person who knew a thing or two about speed. Prior to the war, he had been a championship racecar driver. He had won the Indianapolis 500 in 1925 in the first race at the historic track in which the winner averaged more than 100 miles per hour. He later became a top winning driver in races throughout Europe. When he knocked on Yeager's hotel room that night in Geneva, he was serving as a lieutenant colonel in the US Army, and he was the Army Air Forces' air attaché in Switzerland.

Over a nice meal, DePaolo explained that Yeager's unique experience as an evader in France, then crossing the Pyrenees into neutral Spain, made him a good candidate to assist with a knotty problem that required a workable solution. At the time, there were about 800 downed American flyers hiding out in Switzerland and about 1,600 more stuck in Spain. Now, the US

Army and the American consulates in both countries were trying to figure a way to smuggle all those men out and get them back home. Neither neutral country was willing to do much to help in the effort. Germany would see that as a hostile act. Especially considering the mood of Adolf Hitler in those desperate days, they might well be attacked if he felt they had betrayed their neutrality in any way. It was a very touchy situation.

Yeager admitted to DePaolo that he was a better fighter pilot than he was a diplomat. Or human smuggler. But for the next week he assisted in planning how to get those airmen evacuated out of Switzerland without attracting the attention of the Third Reich. Most of his suggestions relied on plain common sense. As it turned out, Yeager's experiences did help in developing a plan.

First off, he knew there would be no way to escape across the Alps. Not at those altitudes and in the weather they could expect that late in the year. The Pyrenees had been problematic enough and that had been in the springtime. There was no other feasible ground route out of Switzerland.

His suggestion was to take some shot-up American planes that had been forced to land in Switzerland, get them repaired, paint over their US Army Air Forces markings, and use them to fly the men out and to friendly territory. Everyone seemed to like the plan, and preparations were begun to implement it.

Yeager was set to head back home. He would later assume that the scheme was never executed. At least, not that he ever heard. History would come up with the very best solution. The war ended only five months later.

However, his time in Geneva gave Yeager plenty to talk

about for the rest of his life. First was meeting Peter DePaolo and swapping stories with the famous racer. Then there was spending time in the beautiful city and country, ensconced in a nice hotel, but the bed was so much softer than his sleeping bag on a wire rack in Leiston, he spent most nights in Geneva on the floor.

But there was also the interesting return trip. Once back in Lyon, where his P-51 awaited him, all gassed up and ready to go, he ran into an officer in the Office of Strategic Services (OSS, the American foreign intelligence agency), who was also headed back to England. He complained to Yeager that he would have to wait several more hours for his scheduled ride to show up.

"If you don't mind sitting in my lap, I can have you there in time for supper," Yeager told the intelligence officer.

The man only had to consider the offer for a few seconds. Something told him it would be quite the adventure to fly home in a Mustang piloted by a bona fide fighter ace.

An adventure, yes, but it was cramped in the Mustang's cockpit. Plus, the OSS officer also had to fly with cargo on his lap. A case of champagne. To make it a bit roomier, Yeager kept the plane's canopy open, which required they remain at a relatively low altitude.

That made it a chilly ride, but at least it kept the champagne cool.

EIGHTEEN

OLD CROW, OLD OVERHOLT, AND *GLAMOROUS GLEN*

The best example of the combined use of air and ground troops that I ever witnessed.

—US Army general George S. Patton on the
Battle of the Bulge, December 1944–January 1945

The Battle of the Bulge took place from December 16, 1944, to, officially, January 25, 1945, with brutal fighting among the beautiful but thick forests of the Ardennes region of Belgium and Luxembourg. Hitler's aim in ordering what amounted to a last-ditch offensive was to try to stop the Allies from making use of the valuable port of Antwerp. He also believed—although his top generals tried to dissuade him of the notion—that his army could swoop in quickly, drive a wedge into the Allied lines, then surround and hopefully kill as many troops as possible. Then the SS could capture the prime seaport. The ultimate game would be to convince the Allies to sign a favorable peace treaty, ending the threat from the west.

After reaching that peace settlement, Hitler believed he could then demand that the Russians halt their devastating advance from the east. It was the ploy of a desperate madman, and it would result in one of the bloodiest battles of World War II. German field marshal Walther Model was one of Hitler's top commanders. He dared to caution Hitler against launching the offensive. Shortly before the attack began, Model confided to subordinates that Hitler's plan "hasn't got a damned leg to stand on" and "has no more than a ten percent chance of success."

It would also end up being the final major offensive by the Axis powers, and Chuck Yeager and his squadron would play a role in assuring it was ultimately a failure for the Third Reich. Afterward and for the next five months, Hitler's military would be in retreat. However, the Battle of the Bulge was especially brutal. Men died in snowy foxholes from artillery shells. Many of those who were captured by the enemy were executed on the spot by SS units rather than taken prisoner. The bitter cold and icy conditions claimed the lives of other soldiers. More than 15,000 Allied troops suffered what the Army called "cold injuries," such as pneumonia and frostbite.

From the first days of the offensive, it appeared the SS might be successful. That was primarily because cloudy skies during the first week of the battle prevented air cover. That gave the Germans the opportunity to set and fire their artillery and to maintain routes to bring in supplies and ammunition for the troops as well as shells for their big guns. They were able to keep up an almost constant barrage toward the Allied troops. It also prevented reconnaissance by air, which allowed the Germans to begin the battle with a massive and successful surprise attack from multiple fronts, pushing the Allies back.

But the skies cleared on Christmas Eve, 1944. That bit of

good fortune for the Allies—and what many considered a "Christmas miracle" and answered prayers—changed the course of the battle. American aircraft, including the P-51s of the 363rd Fighter Squadron of the Eighth Air Force, could finally see what they were shooting at and determine where the Germans' emplacements, troops, and supply routes were. General George Patton, who commanded the Third Army after D-Day and played a major role in the Battle of the Bulge, gave high praise to the Allied aircraft for their part in the eventual victory. He called it "the best example of the combined use of air and ground troops that I ever witnessed."

Many years later, Vernon Brantley, a veteran of the battle, told a newspaper reporter, "It was on that bright, clear and cold Christmas morning in 1944 that the ground froze solid. The tanks and air forces could finally maneuver and get assistance to all of us who were previously blocked off. It was a welcome sign to see the sun come up. It meant that we were alive for one more day."

Between Chuck Yeager's secret trip to Switzerland and his final eight missions flown in January, he led his wing mates on several bombing and strafing runs over the Ardennes. When Patton's Third Army rescued beleaguered Allied troops in Bastogne two days after Christmas, the German offensive was essentially over. Even so, fighting continued another month. A delusional Hitler refused to acknowledge defeat, nor would he order an end to the battle and pull back SS forces.

That only led to more casualties on both sides, even though the battle had clearly been won by the Allies well before the new year. The Germans lost more than 100,000 killed. At the peak, the United States had more than 600,000 troops involved. There were about 89,000 American casualties and more than 100,000 among all Allied troops involved. Nineteen thousand US troops lost their lives. Most historians consider the Battle of the Bulge to be the largest and most deadly single battle of World War II and the second largest campaign, exceeded only by the Battle of Normandy beginning on D-Day.

Among his last runs, Chuck Yeager flew several dangerous missions in support of the troops on the ground in the bloody conflict. Those missions—and his World War II exploits—would finally come to a close on January 15, 1945, a couple of weeks before the Battle of the Bulge was officially declared to be over.

That last World War II action for Yeager as well as for his best friend, Bud Anderson, started out just like the previous five dozen had. An early wake-up call, a briefing with a paltry breakfast, a bicycle ride out to the flight line, climbing up into his Mustang's cockpit, and, finally, getting airborne and rendezvousing with the rest of the squadron before heading eastward to do that day's job. This particular mission was typical as well. Not a strafing or bombing run this time, though. Instead, they were to meet up with and escort bombers bound for Leipheim, a town in the southern German region of Bavaria. It was there that the Luftwaffe was building and testing the Messerschmitt Me 262 Swallow jet-powered fighters.

Both men would later admit to a noticeable case of nerves. That short-timer thing again. But once they were up there, flying in tight formation above the heavy bombers, all that faded. Yeager and Anderson had been designated as "spares." That meant they trailed the pack across the English Channel and, if none of the other Mustangs experienced any problems and needed to turn back, they were free to reverse course and go back to base. It was common practice to allow any pilot flying his final run to be a spare.

None of the planes experienced any issues. However, neither Yeager nor Anderson wanted it all to come to a close that way. Since they had no specific orders and were on their own, they quickly decided not to fly back so ingloriously across the Channel and spend the rest of a boring day napping. No, they should do something they could eventually tell their grandkids about.

Yeager, of course, led the way and Anderson—in his plane named *Old Crow*, after his favorite Kentucky bourbon—blindly but happily followed his best friend. He would later admit he had no idea where Yeager was going but he figured it would be interesting and fun.

Their first destination on a cold, clear winter morning turned out to be Switzerland, where Yeager had been only a few weeks before. Near the beautiful peak of Mont Blanc, both pilots jettisoned their wing fuel tanks, and once they had fallen to the ground, the buddies began to use them for target practice. In the process, they zoomed up and down deep valleys and sparred with sheer rock walls. Anderson would later report that their aim was less than perfect that day and they never did set the fuel tanks on fire, much as they tried.

Next, Yeager led his buddy to Geneva to show him the hotel where he had stayed over Christmas and the restaurant where he had dined with Peter DePaolo. But Yeager pointed out those sites in his own unique way: buzzing them at nearly 500 miles per hour and coming so close that they could see the flying snow as their propellers blew it off the rooftops. Doing such a thing in a neutral country in the middle of a world war would almost certainly result in some sort of bad outcome for the perpetrators, but Yeager apparently did not care. He remained determined to make the most of his final mission.

He was not finished with his guided tour for his friend, either. Soon they were over the South of France and Yeager was pointing out some of the significant landmarks that played a role in his rescue by the Maquis. Then he was able to locate the woodsman's shack in the Pyrenees on the edge of the Spanish border. It was the place where he and Pat Patterson had come under fire from the SS troops and had to bail out the back window and into the snow. The convenient log flume was not visible, it was covered with snowdrifts.

Then it was back north, to Paris, a place neither pilot had ever been. They had only seen the city from 35,000 feet while escorting bombers. Well, they were determined to get a closer look this time. They flew low and even buzzed the famous Arc de Triomphe and the Champs-Élysées.

Indeed, the men had quite the day. But when they finally got back to Leiston, it was well past sundown and around 6:00 p.m. Once on the ground, they learned they were the last to return of the ones who had left early that morning. Everyone had been worried about them, afraid they had run into trouble on the way home and might have been shot down. Then, when the ground crew noticed all the searing and black blotches on their wings and around their gun barrels from their attacks on their discarded fuel tanks, they immediately assumed these two aces had participated in one hell of a dogfight over there.

After all, the rest of the squadron—the ones who had flown on after parting company with their two "spares"—had encountered a massive force of German fighters along the way. The air-to-air fighting had been wild, with the Mustangs claiming at least five dozen Luftwaffe aircraft. Now, with Yeager and Anderson returning late, and with *Glamorous Glen III* and *Old Crow* showing such obvious signs of combat, everyone assumed the two aces had an even more spectacular story to tell.

Nope. Anderson later wrote that the big battle they missed had occurred at about the same time he and Yeager were in neutral Switzerland trying to set their dropped fuel tanks afire near Mont Blanc. The two aces were so upset about missing all the fun that they promptly went back to their quarters and got falling-down drunk on the rationed whiskey they had been saving. After each mission, the Army Air Forces issued each returning pilot a small portion of a booze called Old Overholt. Yeager and Anderson had been saving theirs for one last celebration after their last run. It was actually nasty stuff. During the war, Old Overholt and other American whiskey distilleries had been ordered to switch their facilities to manufacture industrial alcohol instead. Those who continued to make drinking whiskey had to cut corners, even on the stuff the military bought to issue to pilots, soldiers, and sailors as "medicinal alcohol."

Still, it served its purpose that night in Leiston. They managed to completely forget one fact. Had they been there with the rest of their squadron that day and taken part in that huge air battle, they could just as easily have been killed on their final mission.

Anderson, who was promoted to the rank of major toward the end of 1944—at the ripe old age of twenty-two—would complete his service in the war as a triple ace and with sixteen and one-quarter confirmed kills. He was the top pilot in his squadron after serving two tours in Europe and flying 116 combat missions, but he was one of the few to never have his airplane struck by enemy fire. Not a single bullet.

In Yeager's sixty-one missions, he received credit for an impressive eleven and a half kills and earned double-ace status. Although he had been only a private in the Army not that long before, and he never dreamed he could become an officer when he signed up to become an airplane mechanic, he would go home as a captain in the Army Air Forces.

He did not, however, head directly home. Not back to West Virginia, that is. Instead, he went all the way back to California with Anderson, who had grown up near San Francisco. It was there, on the Anderson family ranch, that Yeager spent his twenty-second birthday on February 13, 1945. He celebrated with a cake Bud's mother baked for him. But the next day he was off to collect his bride-to-be, Glennis Dickhouse, and then head back east to introduce her to his family and to get married.

It is not clear why, but the double wedding ceremony Yeager and Anderson had planned never took place. Clarence "Bud" Anderson would marry his fiancée, Eleanor Cosby, in a separate ceremony a month later. He would go on to a long career in the

Air Force and eventually retire as a colonel after being decorated more than two dozen times for his service to his country.

Chuck Yeager, accustomed to giving orders, showed up at Glennis Dickhouse's home, gave her a hug and a kiss, and told her to pack her bags. When she asked him why, he simply said, "Why do you think?"

He had still not proposed marriage to her. But she was thrilled that the "foregone conclusion" she anticipated was really going to happen. One clue during his year in England was that he sent her just about all of the money he earned, asking her to put it in the bank "for us."

Soon they were on the train from San Francisco, bound for little Hamlin, West Virginia. Glennis would later write that she felt like she was going to a foreign country, based on the thick accents of her future in-laws on those few telephone calls they had exchanged. Also, based on the descriptions of the geography of the area Chuck had given her. But that did not matter. She was thrilled she was about to be a military pilot's wife, even with all the frustrations such a life might entail. That included the possibility that he might be stationed at some remote base somewhere, one to which she might or might not be allowed to follow him. She loved Chuck Yeager, though, and was looking forward to a long and interesting life with a very unique man.

Chuck, for his part, was just as thrilled. Many other returning servicemen were finding their prewar romances had not endured the long separation and haunting unknowns. Glennis was just as he remembered her, and he could not be happier about spending the rest of his life with her. Thankfully, and despite his not ever bothering to propose, she still felt the same about him.

But Yeager was not so sure about the rest of his immediate future in the Air Force. He would soon find out exactly what it would be. And where. And it would send him even farther down a path that would make him a household name and one of his nation's most renowned aviators.

NINETEEN

MACH 1

We didn't know if we could break the sound barrier. But it was our duty to try. That's the way I looked at it. Now you've got guys in space vehicles, smoking along at thousands of miles per hour. Speed is relative.
—Chuck Yeager in *Esquire* magazine,
December 2008

The young couple stayed with Chuck's family—in separate bedrooms, of course—once they got to Hamlin. Both were surprised to learn that Chuck was a local hero. The county newspaper had written at length about his heroics in the war, and Glennis admitted that was the first she had heard about any of it. Before they could even get their bags unpacked, the people of Hamlin held a huge homecoming parade through the middle of town and a social in the high school gymnasium.

The townsfolk were so proud of Yeager and his bride-to-be that they showered them with gifts, including a set of sterling silver. Glennis knew these people had little money and was gratified by their generosity. She knew immediately that she would love them. Even if she could not understand much of what they said.

They were married in the parlor of the Yeager family home on February 26, 1945, followed by a brief reception. They spent their wedding night at a hotel in Huntington, West Virginia, and then were up early to get right back on a train bound for the West Coast. Finally, they would have time together, alone, for a two-week honeymoon in Del Mar, California, where the Air Force had a rest-and-recreation facility. But the first people they saw when they went down to the beach were Bud Anderson and his new wife, Eleanor.

Somehow the best friends had failed to share with each other their postnuptial plans. Still, everyone was happy about the situation and for the girls to get to know each other.

They also soon learned Chuck and Bud would be moving on to their next duty station together. They were headed for Perrin Field in Denison, Texas, between Dallas and Oklahoma City. As with several other bases where Yeager served, the land for Perrin had been purchased by the city to try to attract some kind of government facility as the military geared up for potential war. In early 1941, Denison was sure they had landed a munitions factory, but that fell through. Local officials determined the site would make a perfect flight training base, and that was what they soon secured. Construction began just about the time Pearl Harbor was bombed. The field was named for a test pilot, Colonel Elmer D. Perrin, who died in the crash of a B-26 bomber on a check-out run near Baltimore in the summer of 1941.

Perrin Field became one of the primary locations for basic pilot training, especially for the increasing need for them in the

Pacific theater. In all, Perrin would graduate more than 10,000 pilots during the war years. And in March of 1945, Anderson and Yeager were sent there to train some of them.

Eleanor rode down in the car with the guys while Glennis went back up to Oroville to collect her things. She then joined Chuck in Texas. When she got there, she could tell at once that Chuck was in a foul mood. Housing was almost nonexistent, and they would have to rent a room in a private home with only limited kitchen access.

His job was not going well, either. He and Bud encountered a great deal of jealousy from the other instructors and commanders who had spent most of the war there in the flatlands of North Texas. They resented the hotshot aces who had been dropped into their midst. And what they considered to be their arrogance, too.

The students did not like them, either. The two experienced pilots were exacting, demanding the best of men they were going to certify to go off and join a shooting war. Yeager and Anderson also tended to get a bit wild in the air, clipping the top limbs out of the few trees that grew in the area, unrolling toilet paper out of the trainer and cutting it up with their wings, buzzing cows and horses and a few ranchers and farmers, and even staging mock dogfights with each other. Student pilots either passed out or lost their breakfasts or both during such high jinks. Some even refused to go back up with those two rowdy instructors.

To make matters worse, both Glennis and Eleanor learned they were pregnant. Their morning sickness did nothing to help the situation. Then yet another change in Army Air Forces procedures came along. But the policy shift helped propel Chuck Yeager to a big military career upgrade.

Out of the blue came a new regulation that pertained to any military personnel who had been prisoners of war or evadees in enemy-occupied territory. Anyone who qualified would be able to select any available assignment at the base of his choice. It took Yeager about a second to decide he would pick any other place besides Perrin Field, Texas. As he hastily completed the necessary paperwork, he sat down on the bed in their little rented room and studied a map of the United States.

Since Glennis was pregnant, they decided it would be best if they were somewhere within reasonable distance of Chuck's family so they could help as needed. That eliminated all the bases across the western United States where he had been stationed during his training days. Easily the closest air base to Hamlin, West Virginia, was Wright Field in Dayton, Ohio. That would be his choice.

When Yeager arrived and reported for duty, they looked at his service records. They quickly noted that he had been a maintenance crew chief, even as a private, then chief of maintenance in his fighter squadron. He had trained extensively in aircraft maintenance, all before he became an ace fighter pilot in the war. So it appeared he was about to be an airplane mechanic again. Or at least in command of a bunch of them. And in a group that worked with test aircraft and that glamorous breed, the test pilots. He would be the assistant maintenance officer in the fighter test section at Wright.

When Chuck and Glennis waved goodbye to the Andersons and headed for Dayton in July of 1945, they got bad news and good news. The bad news was that because the war was still going on—Hitler had killed himself and Germany had surrendered, ending the war in Europe, but the fighting continued in the Pacific, and the Allies were gearing up for a dreaded invasion of the Japanese Home Islands—there simply was no housing for dependents at the Ohio base. Glennis would have to head on back to Hamlin and move in with her in-laws. The good news was that Chuck had landed in possibly the best spot in the Army Air Forces for a man with his unique skill set.

Wright Field had been formally opened in 1927, only a year after the creation of the Army Air Corps. The Army named the facility for the Wright brothers, Orville and Wilbur, two local bicycle shop owners who had dabbled in early aeronautics. Shortly after the beginning of the war, the base became a key location for air warfare research and development. By 1944 the airfield had grown significantly, consisting of more than three hundred buildings. During the war, significant research continued on airplanes there. The goal was to improve the horsepower of plane engines, their operational range and in-flight maneuverability, the safety features for aircrews, and the effectiveness of the weapons they carried.

Without necessarily intending to, Chuck Yeager had landed in the middle of the Army Air Forces' most intensive R & D efforts. He had seen a bit of it during his brief duty there during his training. However, the amount of work going on there by mid-1945 had grown exponentially, both in numbers and scope. He would soon take advantage of being in the right place at the right time.

As before, part of Yeager's job was to check out any plane that came in for maintenance, including those under development. He soon found he was in charge of two huge hangars filled with all sorts of new and work-in-progress aircraft. He also got to inspect captured aircraft from Germany and Japan. "Check out" and "inspect" meant "fly." And he did.

He was soon selected to fly in air shows, too, demonstrating to the public some of the newer aircraft the Army Air Forces had developed, all to boost morale, sell war bonds, and convince Congress of the value of taxpayer money being invested in such weaponry. But the air show assignment came much to the chagrin of the test pilots there at Wright. They felt they should have drawn that duty, because Chuck Yeager was not a test pilot. And never would be, because he was not an engineer with a college diploma to prove it.

In September, after the dropping of the atomic bombs on Hiroshima and Nagasaki and the Japanese surrender, Yeager was dispatched to Muroc Army Airfield—soon to be renamed Edwards Air Force Base—in California's high desert. There, back in familiar territory, he was to help develop service and maintenance procedures for and—when he had time—test-fly the new P-80A Shooting Star airplane. That was America's first operational jet fighter. The aircraft had already had its issues. America's top ace fighter pilot in World War II, Major Richard Bong, had been killed the previous month in a crash while taking off for a test flight in a P-80.

Back at Wright, Colonel Albert Boyd, the commander of the flight test division, was busy putting together his pet program, a training school for Army Air Forces test pilots. Boyd is considered a visionary, because he understood how important airpower would be in any future wars. He knew that one of the best deterrents to nations who were bent on muscling in on the territories of others and torching off another war, regional or global, was to meet such aggression with a strong force from the skies. Boyd would handpick the first class of future test pilots who would help create and develop that force.

One of the first chosen was Chuck Yeager. While he was thrilled to be chosen, he was still worried about whether or not he could manage the highly technical classes that he would be required to complete. It was that no-college-education thing again.

He would later say, "My flying was so good they took mercy on my academics." And, of course, Yeager successfully completed and graduated from the test pilot program.

Along the way, he had heard talk of one key element the Army wanted to address. To reach the kind of air superiority for the United States that Boyd and others were aiming to achieve, they needed to develop an aircraft capable of exceeding the speed of sound. Faster and faster aircraft would assure the kind of dominance necessary to try to prevent war. And then, should it come, to win it.

That was a problem. The sound barrier is the sudden increase in aerodynamic drag that happens when an object approaches the speed of sound—about 760 miles per hour at sea level but closer to 660 miles per hour at the altitude where tests were to be conducted, also known as "Mach 1." The instant an aircraft's speed exceeds the speed of sound, it is said to have broken the sound barrier. At that time, in mid-1947, many scientists and aeronautical engineers believed the resulting shock wave would tear apart any aircraft. Nothing, they said, would ever be able to fly that fast.

Despite all the naysayers, work was already underway out there in California at Muroc Field and at other long-runway facilities around the country. The goal was to develop an aircraft that would challenge that dangerous and possibly impenetrable barrier. Then to use that knowledge to develop warplanes that could consistently do so.

At that time the civilian defense contractors working on new airplanes had their own test pilots. Army test pilots typically did not fly newer aircraft until they were on the verge of being introduced into the fleet.

That was the case with Bell Aircraft, who had the contract to design, test, and deliver the X-1 rocket-powered craft. This would be the plane that would prove—or disprove—that the speed barrier could be safely and consistently surpassed. But, as noted earlier, the civilian Bell pilot demanded a $150,000 bonus for ultimately flying the experimental craft beyond Mach 1. The Army felt their own test pilots were just as well qualified to complete the task in the X-1.

For the first time, the newest service branch, the US Air Force (established September 18, 1947), took on the role of testing developmental aircraft, wresting that task away from the military contractors and their test pilots. Now the first big choice under this new and controversial plan would have to be made. And Colonel Albert Boyd chose high school graduate and World War II ace pilot Chuck Yeager to be the first one to fly the X-1 while attempting the Air Force's most ambitious and dangerous task yet.

Yeager was thrilled, not only for the important flying he would be doing but also because it would put him near the Sierra Nevada Mountains, which he had grown to love in the time he had previously spent in the region. Hunting was good there. So was fishing. And an extra benefit was that Glennis would be returning to a spot very near her home and her mother, who could help her with their growing family while Chuck was up there trying to make sonic booms. In his book, *Press On! Further Adventures in the Good Life*, Yeager would write, "I had seriously wondered if my combat experience hadn't been an impossible act to follow, if perhaps the rest of my life was going to be one long let-down. But in 1945, I had a new career as a test pilot at Muroc and those mountains to explore. Both gave me fresh challenges that might well have been my salvation."

Yeager was well aware of the effects on aircraft approaching Mach 1. In a later interview he talked about the "nuisance" of sometimes being pummeled by a shock wave during dogfights, even in those propeller-driven fighters. In sharp dives, and at 30,000 feet or so altitude, they could get close enough to Mach 1 to cause issues.

"In World War II, in combat in P-51s, we became exposed to the effects of the speed of sound on our airplanes," Yeager explained in a later interview. "A Mustang, a P-47, or any of the other fighters that we were using, the fastest they would go was about 80 percent the speed of sound. They had very thick wings and canopies. The distance air had to travel to go around that wing that's going at about 80 percent of the speed of sound brought its relative velocity to the skin of the wing up to the speed of sound. When this happened a shock wave formed on the thickest part of the wings and the canopy. Behind these shock waves was turbulent air, and your airplane would shake and buffet. It wasn't a hazard. It was just a nuisance if you were trying to track some guy at high speed."

Despite Boyd's unshakable confidence in Yeager, it was a debatable pick. Yeager was no engineer. He had struggled with some of the more esoteric concepts in test pilot training. But Boyd would consistently defend his choice. He liked Yeager's "instinctive flying": "The most instinctive pilot I have ever seen," Boyd maintained. He had witnessed Yeager diagnose problems in an aircraft, literally "on the fly," and prevent crashes. That included watching in person as Yeager put the P-80A Shooting Star through its paces out at Muroc.

The fighter ace also remained remarkably calm and focused in even the most tense situations. There would be no time for panic at 700 miles per hour when it might appear his airplane was about to be battered to pieces by the sound barrier shock wave. And Boyd was also certain that Yeager's unique understanding of the mechanics of an aircraft would allow him to work with the engineers and scientists to report exactly what he was experiencing with the plane while in flight, how adjustments helped or hindered how well the craft flew, and even suggest things they might try. That sort of input was exactly what would be necessary to break through a sonic barrier that had both baffled and spooked scientists and pilots.

He also had another unique but not quite so glamorous qualification. He was very familiar with how high-pressure gas behaved. That came from working as a boy with his father in those coal mine gas fields back in West Virginia. "I was intimately familiar with the diaphragms they used to control 6,000 pounds of pressure in the wells back home," he would later explain. "And the X-1 used that same 6,000 pounds of gas pressure, something I'd worked on as a kid. And I obviously could fly. I was not only a pilot. I knew what the hell was going on mechanically."

Yeager promptly named the Bell X-1 *Glamorous Glennis*, of course. This time, though, he could actually show his wife the paint job on the aircraft's nose. Glennis had moved out to California to be with him now that their son, Donald, had been born.

The X-1 was hung beneath a B-29 bomber, designed to be dropped away at altitude and then have its rocket engine ignited, making the bird essentially into a Roman candle. And once the rockets had used up their fuel—liquid oxygen and alcohol, but only enough for a few minutes' power—or were extinguished by the pilot, she became little more than a glider.

She had to be hauled skyward by the bomber, because the craft's landing gears could not support the weight of the plane when loaded with fuel, plus the plane was simply too heavy to get off the runway. Also, if the flight was aborted and more than half of the fuel remained aboard, the pilot would have to jettison the fuel tanks before attempting a landing. Otherwise the gears would collapse on touchdown and that would be catastrophic.

Yeager and the test team at Muroc flew several glide flights before finally using the rocket power on the fourth run, on August 29, 1947, taking it to Mach 0.85. It was a very rough ride and he almost lost control of the X-1 before finally being able to make the usual unpowered, dead-stick landing back onto the long lake bed runway at Muroc. The calm demeanor Boyd had recognized in Yeager certainly came into play that day. A pilot with less poise and inherent cool might well have augered in.

Did Yeager believe it was possible to break the sound barrier? Did he have doubts about even attempting such a feat? In an appearance in later years before a group of young people at the Academy of Achievement, he was asked those questions. His answers spoke volumes about a sense of duty and having the resolve to do the job, whatever it might be or how likely it was to be a success.

"Well, it's not a matter of thinking it's possible. It's duty," he replied. "It's just like flying combat. If it is [impossible], that's the way it goes. The same way with flying the X-1. It didn't make any difference to me whether I thought the airplane would go faster than sound. I was assigned as a test pilot on it, and it was my duty to fly it. That's the way most military pilots look at it."

Yeager was actually more confident in the possibility of exceeding the barrier than he admitted. The Bell test pilot had consistently gotten the aircraft up to Mach 0.8 already. Yeager would later say, "They were at 80% but they weren't finding out anything. Hell, we had just fought the war at point-eight-Mach. That was top speed on Mustangs [in a dive]. I figured we could work on modifying the X-1 and then we could take her super-sonic."

He also noted that for him, the X-1 was a "fly-twice-a-week" aircraft. Even now, few know that breaking the sound barrier in the rocket-powered plane was only one of Chuck Yeager's jobs at Muroc. He was also flying other aircraft for test-and-development purposes, sometimes several different planes each day, at the same time the Mach 1 project was going on.

After making more changes to the X-1's horizontal tail, as suggested by engineers, and with Yeager agreeing that he could change the angle of attack in small increments as he approached Mach 1, *Glamorous Glennis* could likely break right on through that hellish speed bump. They only needed to keep tweaking until they proved it once and for all.

Adjustments were made to the craft's control systems, and on October 14 they tried again. Despite those cracked ribs from his horseback-riding accident two nights prior, Yeager dropped away from the B-29, fired all four chambers of his engine in rapid sequence, and bolted away from the launch bomber. As the plane climbed quickly, he shut down two chambers and tested the movable tail he was about to employ for the first time. Meanwhile, his Machmeter registered numbers of 0.83, 0.88, and 0.92, with 1.00 indicating Mach 1.

Now, with the pilot adjusting the tail movements in such small increments, he seemed to be providing effective control of the X-1. Previously, the craft had begun to buck and shudder violently as it approached the sound barrier.

Yeager reached an indicated Mach number of 0.92 as he leveled out at 42,000 feet. It was time. He restarted a third chamber of his engine. With that additional thrust, the X-1 rapidly accelerated to Mach 0.98.

Later, in his "9th Powered Flight" official report, Yeager would calmly record, "The needle of the machmeter fluctuated at this reading momentarily, then passed off the scale." He did not know just how fast he was going but he knew it was speedier than sound travels. That was his goal. He kept the X-1 at that velocity—whatever it was—for about twenty seconds before shutting off all three of the rockets.

There had been light buffeting as he approached Mach 1 and then again as he slowed to below that barrier. Those on the ground heard the sonic boom. That thunder set off raucous cheers. They knew Yeager had done it. Now all he needed to do was bring the X-1 safely back to earth.

"The flight was concluded by the subsequent glide and a normal landing in the lake bed," he would later write in his report. His calm account made it sound like just another day's airplane ride high over the desert. From the time he dropped away from the B-29 until he was wheels-down on Mother Earth, the entire trip took only fourteen minutes. But it was fourteen minutes that changed the course of modern aviation and once again made Charles E. Yeager a hero. It also gave him the moniker of the "Fastest Man Alive." At least he would be awarded that nickname in June of 1948, almost a year after the historic achievement. That was when enough of the details were ultimately declassified for the world to know what he and the X-1 team had accomplished.

It would also earn him the Collier Trophy, presented annually "for the greatest achievement in aeronautics or astronautics in America, with respect to improving the performance, efficiency, and safety of air or space vehicles." In presenting the award, the National Aeronautic Association called Yeager's feat "an epochal achievement in the history of world aviation—the greatest since the first successful flight of the original Wright Brothers' airplane, forty-five years ago." And he was further honored with the Mackay Trophy, "awarded for the most meritorious flight of the year by an Air Force person, persons, or organization."

That X-1 plane went on display at the Smithsonian Institution in 1950 and millions of visitors have seen it in person since.

Chuck Yeager, who could alternately be quite boastful or off-puttingly self-effacing, depending on his mood, would always describe that momentous short flight as mostly smooth and uneventful. He said it was little more than "poking a hole through Jell-O." In future interviews, he would often compare that historic flight as little more than piloting his P-51 propeller-driven fighter into steep dives. He maintained that he had already experienced the effects the X-1 test pilots were facing in that bird way back when he was chasing Luftwaffe Messerschmitts in dogfights over Germany.

He would also downplay a subsequent attempt to take a later version of the rocket plane through Mach 2 and approach 2.5 times the speed of sound. Once past Mach 2 and approaching Mach 3 at 70,000 feet, the plane suddenly began a violent spin, one that required every instinctive bit of flying of which Yeager was capable. He somehow survived up to 9 g's of gravity, thanks to his pressurized suit, and he managed to get the aircraft under control. But even then he had to do some fancy flying just to get the plane down from 25,000 feet and back onto the lake bed runway safely.

He would later tell an interviewer, "When this happened, I was about fifty miles from Rogers Dry Lake, at 25,000 feet. I was sitting there looking and the pressurization was gone out of the cockpit. Part of the canopy was gone, my suit was inflated, but it had kept me alive. I looked around, I finally spotted the lakebed and turned toward it. And from the time the airplane yawed and ran out of fuel up there at 2.5 Mach number, 'til I popped it out of the spin at 25,000 feet, was only fifty-one seconds. But fifty-one seconds, if you will look at your watch, is a long time. And so, I just glided on back to the base and landed. And that's the last flight I made in the airplane. And we never did take it above about Mach two anymore."

For the rest of his life, one of the questions Yeager was most often asked was if he was scared when he was about to fly the X-1 through and experience the hazards of the sound barrier. His answer was always consistent: "It's not a matter of thinking something is going to be dangerous. It's just like flying combat. On a combat mission, you know someone is probably going to get killed. You just hope it isn't you. If it is, that's the way it goes. It was the same way flying the X-1. It didn't make any difference to me whether I thought the airplane would go faster than the speed of sound or not. I was assigned as a test pilot on it, so it was my duty to fly it."

Regardless his aw-shucks attitude, that initial twenty seconds of flight time past the sound barrier would cement his place in American history as well in pop culture. But Chuck Yeager was not finished yet. After that October day in 1947, he still had almost twenty-eight more years of service to his country in the Air Force yet to go.

And another seventy-three years of rich life left to live. The man who piloted the Bell X-1 past the sound barrier was only twenty-four years old when he did it.

TWENTY

"IF I AUGER IN TOMORROW . . ."

*If I auger in tomorrow, it won't be with a frown on my face.
I've had a ball.*

> —Final words of Chuck Yeager's book *Yeager:*
> *An Autobiography*, July 1985

After returning from World War II as a true hero, then breaking the sound barrier and dominating much of the first reel of the movie *The Right Stuff*, Chuck Yeager soon became a highly sought-after speaker, TV talk show guest, and interviewee. He was, as the newspapers said, "good copy." He seemed to never grow tired of answering the same questions over and over. He had plenty of stories to tell and an entertaining and engaging way of spinning those yarns in his distinctive twang. And he was always willing to offer his opinion on the state of aviation or the military or the world.

But there was one subject that seemed to irritate him when it inevitably came up. He admitted as much in his book and many other times. That was whole concept of the "right stuff." The phrase, the book, or the movie—no matter where it appeared. The implication from both Tom Wolfe's book and the

successful movie was that Yeager and a few of his equally colorful contemporary test pilots were deliberately overlooked by
NASA when they selected the first and subsequent crops of
men to train to become astronauts. And the reason was because
the government decided these men did not have what it took to
fly off into space.

When one interviewer suggested Yeager had not exactly
been thrilled with that aspect of the movie, he replied, "No, the
point was, *The Right Stuff* was not a documentary. It was entertainment. The Air Force came out smelling like a rose, but a lot
of the things that were depicted in that movie were pretty fic-
tional, you might say."

Yeager also pointed out that when the space program actually started in 1959, he had already been promoted to the rank
of colonel and was busy running his own F-86 and then F-100
fighter squadrons, the first in Germany and the latter back at
George Air Force Base in Victorville, California. He loved being
involved once again in tactical-fighting flight. One of the best
things about such duty, in his opinion, was that the young pilots under his command always wanted to challenge their boss,
the "old man," in mock dogfights. That was because he just
happened to be a famous fighter ace and record-breaking pilot.
As it happened, Yeager proceeded to smoke all of them, easily
and every time. That was still the most fun for him, and he
firmly believed flying should, first and foremost, be fun.

It was also true that, despite his obvious abilities as a pilot
and all those infamous exploits of his, he simply did not qualify
to become an astronaut. At least not based on NASA's very

specific and rigid requirements. Besides, he claimed, he never really had any desire to become an astronaut.

"The requirement to get into the space program was to have a degree, preferably in engineering, math or one of the sciences," he later told an interviewer. "I only had a high school education. I didn't give it a thought. I couldn't care less about it because to me it wasn't flying. It was riding in capsules."

Even so, the "right stuff" question would follow him the rest of his days, all the way to an appearance in many versions of his eventual obituary.

Mixed in with several command positions, Yeager somehow found time for another record-breaking attempt. In December of 1963, he was back at Edwards Air Force Base to try to break the altitude mark recently set by the Russians. That was 113,890 feet above sea level. Both his wife and his mother were at the base that day, along with a sizable crowd allowed to observe the test—even though, if he was successful, it would occur almost 22 miles above the desert floor and thus be difficult for those on the ground to see. As it happened, that was probably for the best.

Yeager was piloting a Lockheed NF-104, a jet- and rocket-powered plane easily capable of flying at Mach 2 and reaching high altitudes on the edge of outer space. He quickly drove the airplane to 104,000 feet. He was still climbing with little effort and the record in sight when suddenly the aircraft began spinning wildly. Yeager would later admit he was climbing with the nose at a little too great of an attack angle. But once he was in the spin, he realized he had lost hydraulic pressure and, with it, all control of the aircraft. Despite the tremendous gravity forces as the NF-104 plunged earthward, he managed to hang on and eject from the cockpit only seconds before the plane augered in.

But in the process, his cockpit seat, which he had not yet noticed was on fire, slammed into his face, breaking the rubber seal around his helmet. The pure oxygen inside the helmet ignited before Yeager could get it off, badly burning him. Despite being so close to the ground before he could leave the plane and finding himself occupied with getting the helmet full of fire off his head, he still managed to ride his chute down safely.

Somehow he survived the ordeal but suffered bad burns. After painful procedures to avoid it, he ended up with only minimal scarring. But a scene depicting that fiery event also found its way into the film version of *The Right Stuff*.

After that latest close call, he continued with his Air Force career, taking the opportunity to climb into a cockpit and fly every chance he got. That included commanding five fighter squadrons during the Vietnam War while based in the Philippines. Yeager himself took part in more than 125 missions there.

Later, in 1968, he commanded the 4th Tactical Fighter Wing—an F-4 Phantom jet fighter unit—that was deployed to South Korea during the USS *Pueblo* crisis. From there, he would sometimes climb into a plane and dash down to Vietnam to visit with his son, Mick, who was also in the Air Force at the time, fittingly enough serving as an aircraft mechanic.

In 1969, after a quarter century in the Army Air Corps, then the Army Air Forces, and finally the US Air Force, Chuck Yeager was promoted to the rank of brigadier general. He retired from the Air Force on March 1, 1975. The attendees at his retirement party represented a varied cross section of all types who had crossed paths with Yeager over the years. Bud Anderson was there, of course, and he described the crowd as being made up of "test pilots and generals, fighter pilots and corporate millionaire honchos, and not a few drunks. It was a typical Yeager crowd!"

Yeager was not finished with the Air Force, though. For the huge sum of a dollar a year, he served as a consultant to the service branch, just for the opportunity to fly all the newest aircraft. He also had a consulting contract with Northrup that paid considerably better wages. They also allowed him seat time in most of their newly developed airplanes.

In 2009, Yeager told an interviewer from *Men's Journal*, "I've flown 341 types of military planes in every country in the world and logged about 18,000 hours. It might sound funny, but I've never owned an airplane in my life. If you're willing to bleed, Uncle Sam will give you all the planes you want."

When Tom Wolfe's award-winning and best-selling book was published and the movie *The Right Stuff* premiered—the book in 1979 and the film, which was nominated for eight Oscars and won four, in 1983—they only added to Yeager's legendary status. And gave him the opportunity to take advantage of his associated popularity.

———————

After his retirement, Chuck and Glennis moved to a new home in Grass Valley, California, between Sacramento and the Sierra

Nevada Mountains. It was not far from where Glennis had been born and grown up, and Yeager had grown quite fond of the area. Later, in his book *Press On! Further Adventures in the Good Life*, he said, "I'd seen the Alps and Pyrenees from the air, and I'd watched the sun come up on the Atlantic Ocean, but I was truly taken aback by the spectacular beauty of the Sierras. I guess I had finally found the Shangri La I had been looking for."

They had four children by then, Susan, Don, Mick, and Sharon, who were off living their own lives. From their new home, Chuck and Glennis ran a burgeoning business based on his many speaking and consulting jobs. Despite his opinions about the book and movie, *The Right Stuff* proved a boon for personal appearances, and he was perfectly happy to capitalize on it. Honoraria for speaking engagements were often in the $25,000 range. Commercial endorsements for General Motors and ACDelco and his work with Electronic Arts video games were lucrative as well and only boosted his popularity, his recognizability, and his marketability. That caused the demand for him to speak to reach even greater heights.

In one interview, Yeager claimed to have given 163 speeches in one year. Proceeds from his best-selling autobiography—estimates are that the book has so far earned about $5 million in royalties—helped their finances as well. He still managed to find time to hunt and fish, though, relishing the ability to return to his favorite youthful pastimes. He also took up hang gliding and enjoyed it very much. Meanwhile, Glennis started a successful real estate business there in the foothills of the Sierras.

This new life gave Yeager more time to get to know his kids and grandkids, too. Glennis had said that he was typical of the men of that era. He loved his children, provided for them, but it was the wife's duty to raise them. He was gone so much while in the Air Force, he really had no choice.

Along the way, he was almost continually being approached with various investments, offers, and schemes. He turned practically all of them down. That sort of thing might get in the way of flying, hunting, and fishing. A group of Republicans in West Virginia tried to convince him to run for the US Senate back in his home state against the venerable longtime Democrat, Robert Byrd. That would have pleased Yeager's dad, who had once refused to shake President Harry Truman's hand at an event at which he was giving Chuck the Collier Award for his aeronautical achievements. Why? Simply because Truman was a Democrat. Both the secretary of defense and the secretary of the Air Force were there for the ceremony and thought it was hilarious. Chuck's mother helped defuse that touchy situation by talking with the president, discussing mostly the best way to cook cornbread.

In the end, he and Glennis agreed they could not envision Chuck as a politician. He was much too plainspoken and direct for such a job. His only dabbling in politics was when he appeared in a television commercial for George H. W. Bush's presidential campaign in 1988.

Yeager had always told Glennis, "I've named every plane I fly after you, hon, because you are my good luck charm. Those planes always bring me home to you." Not quite accurate, since the burning wreckage of *Glamorous Glen II* had ended up somewhere in the South of France, but the sentiment was still there. Even though they saw a bit more of each other after his retirement, the marriage remained strong. They were devoted to each other.

In the mid-1980s, Glennis went in for her annual physical examination. Even though she felt fine, she received unexpected bad news. She was diagnosed with ovarian cancer. Like her husband, she decided she would fight this enemy. Fight and win. In his autobiography, Chuck described how she willingly underwent huge amounts of chemotherapy yet still managed, through sheer force of will, to get past the awful side effects without complaint. He equated it with pilots who know things might get tough but are determined to press on. He told his friends that if anyone could beat the disease, it was Glennis.

Indeed, it seemed she had conquered her illness and was eventually pronounced cancer-free. But as so often happens, the disease returned. Her battle ultimately lasted six years.

Glennis Yeager passed away on December 22, 1990, at the base hospital at Travis Air Force Base near Fairfield, California. She was sixty-six years old. They had been married for forty-five years. At the time of her death, she and Chuck had thirteen grandchildren.

Glennis never talked much about *The Right Stuff*, but she did say that her portrayal in the film by actress Barbara Hershey and the steamy way Hershey looked at actor Sam Shepard, who played Chuck, was right on the money. Other things might have been a stretch in the film, but not their love for each other.

With Glennis gone, Chuck threw himself even more into his busy schedule, as well as hunting and fishing. Flying, too. Every chance he got.

In 2000, he was hiking along a trail in Nevada County,

California, when he met an attractive blonde and struck up a conversation. Her name was Victoria Scott D'Angelo, an aspiring actress who had appeared in a small role in the Harrison Ford movie *Witness*. With that on her résumé, she decided to come to Hollywood to seek a career in the movies. Although she was thirty-five years younger than Yeager, the two hit it off, started dating, and were married in August of 2003. Yeager had turned eighty the previous February.

Chuck Yeager died on National Pearl Harbor Remembrance Day, December 7, 2020, in a Los Angeles hospital. He was ninety-seven years old. Despite reports in the media that he had succumbed to Covid-19, no one confirmed it, denied it, or commented on the reports. The cause of death has so far not been made public. Victoria simply announced his passing that night on Yeager's Twitter account feed: "It is w/ profound sorrow, I must tell you that my life love General Chuck Yeager passed just before 9pm ET. An incredible life well lived, America's greatest Pilot, & a legacy of strength, adventure, & patriotism will be remembered forever."

His obituary in the *New York Times* was merely one of many to bring up the "right stuff." That connection and breaking the sound barrier were the primary points mentioned by most who ran stories. "Chuck Yeager, the most famous test pilot of his generation, who was the first to break the sound barrier and, thanks to Tom Wolfe, came to personify the death-defying aviator who possessed the elusive yet unmistakable 'right stuff,' died on Monday in Los Angeles."

Few of them offered much more than a short mention of his remarkable service and heroism during World War II.

Yeager's memorial service was held at the Charleston Coliseum & Convention Center in Charleston, West Virginia, at noon on January 15, 2021. Fighter jets flew overhead through rain clouds to honor him, and there was a twenty-one-gun salute.

Earlier that day, in an interview on a local radio station, his widow said, "Our only arguments were when I would say, 'You're a hero.' And he would say, 'No, I'm not.' He didn't understand any of that because his whole thing was duty. That's what he was told to do and he did it. He appreciated it when people would show appreciation because he did risk his life."

Chuck Yeager was preceded in death not only by Glennis but also by his son Mick (Michael), who had also served in the US Air Force and was visited by his dad while serving during the Vietnam War. Mick died suddenly of an undisclosed cause at the age of sixty-three on March 26, 2011, in Eugene, Oregon.

Early reports after Chuck Yeager's death indicated that the general would be buried at Arlington National Cemetery in Washington, DC. However, a "family member"—likely Victoria— responded in a Twitter post from the "Chuck Yeager" account that that would not be the case. "There is no family there" was the reason cited. "Most likely West Virginia. Per his father's advice, he never forgot where he came from." As of this writing, the details of his interment or cremation, including the location of his remains, have not been made public.

There is a quote on the dust jacket of Chuck Yeager's autobiography that sums up his outlook on life. He says, "'The right stuff' . . . those words seem meaningless when used to describe a pilot's attributes. I don't deny that I was damned good. If there is such a thing as 'the best,' I was at least one of the title contenders. I've had a full life and enjoyed just about every damned minute of it because that's how I lived."

And that seems a perfectly fine epitaph for a true American hero.